This book is written as a tribute to Ivor, Tom, Cooper, Katie and Polly Price.

Ivor, was my husband and best friend.

Tom, Cooper, Katie and Polly are my four children

And greatest teachers

In this thing called life

Katie is the star of the show.

If Katie had not been stillborn there would not be a book.

Katie Price

M.A.D.

She Really

"Made a Difference"

By

Anita Price

New Generation **Publishing**

Contents

Are You Ready?

In each chapter of this book I share my experiences with you. You have a bit of me, sometimes a very private, personal bit that even my closest friends and family may feel they are seeing for the very first time. This is great, but the impact is even greater if you not only read and hear my experiences, but you check to see how they apply in your life.

Give a copy to your friends and families. Give a copy to your work colleagues. Whenever you are talking to someone and that little voice in your head says to share what you know then go for it. The worst that can happen is that they think you are mad. You'll learn from these pages that what other people think really doesn't matter. It is what you know and believe that counts. I know you are ready to work on you. It stands to reason, because you wouldn't be reading this book otherwise. Get going. Get changing…

Don't delay
Do it today.

Believing is seeing

Dream it, do it and discover

Don't simmer
Get cooking.

Begin, believe and become

If it's meant to be
It's up to me.
Reach up for the sky
And we'll meet at the top.

You can eat an elephant
One bite at a time.

The longest journey begins with a single step.

Setting the Scene

Ivor and I have four children. Only two are alive today.

1990 Tom, the size of a thumb nail was flushed down the toilet.

   We had just finished designing and building a house and it all seemed so pointless.

1991 Cooper arrived safely after an emergency caesarian.

1993 Katie was stillborn. We were building yet another house and life, although a total waste of time, had to go on.
Thank God for Cooper!

1994 Polly Kate Price, delivered by caesarian section less than a year after Katie's death / birth.

2001 Moved to live in the centre of the village so Cooper and Polly could be their own people and call for their friends.

2003 Moved to live by the sea to the place we dreamed of retiring.
Retirement brought forward nearly twenty years. Everybody dies but not everybody lives. We live life to the full.

   Thank- you Katie.

2008 I ask Ivor to share his thoughts to be included in the book.

He leaves with one small bag. Having supported each other when Katie ripped our lives apart, surely, nothing can come between us.

2013 The book is born. Safely delivered to the public. I am strong.

I am happy and the book blooms like a rose as a tribute to Baby Katie.

Where to Begin?

Picture the scene, there we are, two adults searching for hidden treasure in the spare bedroom. I guess my husband's idea of treasure and mine are two different things. We need a computer with a floppy drive. The excitement mounts as we unearth the old computer and wait with baited breath to see if it works.

I have two floppy discs in my hand, both labelled "Katie Price." More than ten years ago I typed to ease my grief. I typed to work through my anger as I firmly believe that the only way out of pain is to work through it. I was hurting and some sections were just too painful to write.

That was ten years ago and I am now seeing the contents of the floppy disc on the screen. Like baby Katie, the discs have been buried – out of sight but not out of mind. I can't believe I actually typed some of this. Even more surprising, what I am reading is making me smile. All I could do was cry when Katie was stillborn on 13th September 1993. I know they say that time heals, but, it truly does. The wounds are no longer raw but baby Katie is never far from my thoughts.

I read from the screen. ...
Are things what they seem?

I am sitting up in bed looking at our brand – new baby girl sleeping peacefully in her Moses basket. She was sleeping but I desperately wanted to hold her close to me. You don't pick up babies when they are asleep, do you? When they sleep you should have your rest. I agonised over the decision for a whole two seconds before struggling out of bed to pick her up. If you've had stitches you'll remember how it feels. She weighed in at six pounds two ounces and still I started to tear. I am radiant when I am pregnant but I am not very good with the delivery bit!

I am sitting up in bed cradling my daughter in my arms. Her hair is dark, her cheeks are flushed and her lips are dark red. She is wearing a plain white baby-grow with a white satin collar. The silence of the room is deafening when the Doctor, a group of students, a nurse and the ward sister enter. They are doing their rounds. Things are not what they seem. I have been caught in the act of cuddling baby Katie. Why should I feel guilty? She is my daughter and our time together is limited. They need to take her away. They need to carry out the post mortem. They need to find out exactly why she died. I can feel myself blushing. I feel embarrassed; they'll think I am mad cuddling a dead baby. I really don't care what they think. This is my daughter that we are talking about, and I need to hold her. I need the fact that I have actually delivered a baby to sink into my brain. Have I really had a baby girl? Are they really talking to me? I can understand that they are talking to me about the funeral arrangements but the word contraception has tumbled into the conversation. I have just lost my precious baby – why would I want to avoid getting pregnant again? I want a baby. I don't want any old baby! I want to feed; hug and just love baby Katie. I couldn't possibly think about "nooky" right now and maybe never again. I'm in a single, hospital bed for goodness sake. Another pregnancy is too painful to think about and too scary, too everything. Can't people understand that there is a huge gap and the only way to ease that hurt is to lie in my husband's arms in the privacy of our home and to hold my son, Cooper. I don't want to talk about the funeral, contraception, the post mortem. I just don't want to talk but, I know, they are just doing their job.

The Sister has spoken; my thoughts are interrupted. She repeats her question "May I hold her?" She says it so tenderly that it makes me cry and with pride I pass baby Katie to her. Maybe they wouldn't think I'm silly for cuddling her. She is on loan to me for such a short time. If this is counted in breaths instead of seconds and minutes it is no time at all. No breaths, just a few brief cuddles and a shed full of tears and heartache.

Things aren't always what they seem in the midst of life and death. It is all down to how we perceive a particular situation. I work with students and I often tell students the story of the father and son who are out driving one day when they have a serious accident. The father is killed and the son is seriously injured. He is taken to the local hospital and a surgeon is brought into Casualty to look at him. The surgeon takes one look at the boy and says "I can't operate, it's my son." How can this be? Think about it for a minute. Some people assume that the surgeon is a man, just like the Doctor doing his rounds and the female nurse who asked to hold Katie. In this world of equal opportunities why shouldn't the surgeon be the boy's mum?

Things are the same the world over. Do you know the story of Johnny who didn't want to go to school one day. His Mother explained that he would see all his friends and, anyway it was Friday so he would have the weekend to chill and do his own thing. He still sat crumpled in a heap and didn't attempt to move so she came down a little harder and said "Look Johnny, you have to go to school, you are the head- master!"

I wonder how the Doctors and nurses on "that" ward round felt on 14th September 1993. Were they keen to go to work or did they understand how Johnny felt? Did they wish they were somewhere else when they were given the notes for the patient in "The Swallow Suite". The double bedroom with tea and coffee making facilities that is used for bereaved parents. Katie arrived in the middle of the night and Ivor wasn't sent home. Instead we were shown to our room. There was no balcony and the sun didn't shine in the morning. It rained and there was no rainbow. Our room was separate from the maternity ward and there was no hint of a cry. It would have been too painful. It was when Ivor returned from his quest for the gents toilet that the ward round were in deep discussion. I would be allowed home later that day. I refused to leave until I saw the consultant who had helped me through the period of post natal depression I had suffered after Cooper was born. The hospital staff were brilliant. I saw the consultant, arranged a follow up appointment with him for the next week and we left the hospital that afternoon. My arms ached with emptiness, my heart was heavy and my eyes were so blurred I could hardly see through my tears. Ivor was a tower of strength as he led me outside and into the safety of our car. I didn't suffer with depression after Katie's birth and I believe it was because I had done as much as I could to help the grieving process. Thank God that I struggled out of bed to cradle baby Katie in my arms because the very act made me realise that she was real and it really wasn't just a bad dream. It was a nightmare, but I had done my utmost to protect myself.

Several years later I am on a training course. A group of us are talking over coffee. The main topic is our families. Why is it that women love to share the detail of their labours even many years after the event? Suddenly my attention is drawn to a conversation at the other side of the group. I hear a lady saying "My twins were born on 12th September 1993 and one died." I say "Katie was stillborn on 13th September 1993. The nurse had said someone needed "The Swallow Suite." I look at the lady in disbelief, as if seeing a ghost from my past. She gave up the security of The Swallow Suite and her family moved out so we could sleep within the safety of its walls, free from the sight or sound of a new born. She had cuddled her son within those four walls and in the same space we cuddled our baby daughter while she slept peacefully. The course was worthwhile but what I learned at that coffee break will stay with me forever. I was meant to be there that day purely to meet this wonderful lady as we has so much more than our work in common.

In the midst of sadness I have to smile at the thought of Ivor wandering the corridors looking for the gents. When he enters the room the white – coated group sprinkled with blue uniforms agree to take baby Katie. Ivor asks where they will take her. He needs to know that she will be treated with the utmost respect and not stored in a cupboard. The silence is unbearable and in the place of the Moses basket stands a vase of rosebuds and gypsophelia. I have since read that gypsophelia is commonly known as baby's breath. So ironic, as Katie did not breathe our impure air.

This is the only information on the first floppy. At the time you think I would have written about the events leading up to Katie's birth and the delivery itself. It would have been too painful to record my innermost thoughts and feelings at the time. It is certainly true that time is a great healer. Today, looking out of the living room window, into the garden I focus on the pale pink rose buds. The garden looks beautiful but I picture how the same garden looked over a decade ago the day before Katie made her appearance. Surprise, surprise, it was a building site. We were renovating a house in Cardiff. Ivor, Cooper and I lived in a caravan on site. We must have needed our heads examined. Much to the annoyance of the builder Cooper played with his diggers in the sand. When we started the building project we didn't know I was pregnant. We were both thrilled at the prospect of a brother or sister for Cooper. Cooper knew that there would soon be a baby. The builder and his team were working flat out to get the house finished in time for us to bring the new baby home. Lots of hard work and rushing, and all for nothing. The baby's room was not decorated as, in any event, it would remain empty for some time. There was no baby to bring home. Katie was brought to the family home the night before her funeral.

Katie was born on 13 September 1993. No, it wasn't a Friday and no, this isn't a book of doom and gloom. It is based on the positive, uplifting and true story of the Price family. If you have managed to live this long and not experienced real tragedy, then think yourself lucky, because you will not escape forever. Life has a habit of kicking you in the shins and bringing you down to earth with a jolt when you least expect it.

When Katie was stillborn we experienced physical and mental anguish. Why us? Could life ever be good again? Who would steal a baby from its mother's arms? She wasn't kidnapped. If she had, there would have been a chance of getting her back alive. There was no chance of this but, I believe that if you give life a chance life be good again. Why not let it be better than it ever was before! It is as if the trauma of losing Katie changed our perception of life. Things that were so very important at one time seemed to pale into insignificance. My career and material things that can be replaced became irrelevant in the whole scheme of things. It was like putting on a new pair of glasses that allowed me to see things as they truly are for the very first time. The glasses weren't rose -coloured either! Although as you delve deeper into this book you will see that roses have played a significant part in my growth as a person. When you can learn from an experience and ultimately use it to help others this is learning at its best. This is the seed of something bigger than you. Ask yourself which comes first - the apple or the seed? The apple can't grow without the tree and the tree can't grow without the seed. Soon from a single pip you can have a whole orchard.

True learning involves being honest with yourself. We don't know what we don't know or don't understand until we identify the gap and learn from it. The story of the Emperor and the flower seed is about honesty the Emperor was very old and needed a successor. As the Emperor loved nature and flowers in particular, he decided that flowers should help him choose. The Emperor gave every child a flower seed and said that the person who grew the most beautiful flower would be his successor. On the day of judging the great hall of the palace was full of flowers of all shapes and sizes. The Emperor examined each flower carefully. Finally, the Emperor came to one little girl holding nothing but a pot of soil. The Emperor asked "Why did you bring an empty pot child?" "Your Majesty," said the little girl, "I planted the seed you gave me and I watered it every day, but it did not sprout." The seed had been roasted and would not sprout. For her honesty, the little girl was selected to be the Emperor's successor.

Let's call the seed within Katie. I looked after her

and took her on every hospital visit. She grew, she developed and everything was as expected. There was no cause for concern and when she was born she still looked so perfect. Looks can be deceiving. I can't tell you how she did it but she always moved a lot. She must have turned around too much.

She turned around so much
The cord which provided her nourishment
Went around her neck and face
So perfect, so sweet, so silent,
What a waste

That can't be true. She altered my life and I'm sure many others have taken stock of their lives and what is important. Katie certainly planted a seed. Like the seed in the little girl's pot she wasn't meant to grow on earth. She wasn't meant to grow up with me. It makes me wonder which came first, the chicken or the egg? Something or someone else was hatching not long after Katie's appearance.

Certainly a lot of good has come out of the tragedy that hit the Price family on that dreaded September morn. We mourned but something big and new was hatching in the Price family. I don't just mean the fact that Polly Price put in an appearance on 31 August 1994, less than a year after her sister's death! Either way Katie or Polly would have been in the same class in school Katie would have been one of the oldest, or Polly is, without a doubt, the youngest. Try as we might, we were destined to have a daughter in that academic year.

I agonised over the title of this book. The books by Susan Coolidge first came to mind. My first idea was "What Katie Couldn't Do", but she did so much for so many people. I believe one little soul has changed so many lives. Maybe the book should be called "What

Katie Did for Us." It is like throwing a pebble in the water. A small pebble can make big, far- reaching ripples on still water. She was stillborn and Thank- God for her. The day of the funeral the church was overflowing and grown men cried. We will never be sure just how far the ripples of her death have spread and just how many people have taken stock of their own lives. I believe she was born for a purpose. We suffer traumatic experiences for a reason and if we learn from the experience we can go on to fulfill our true destiny.

Why the title Katie Price M. A. D.? Katie wasn't mad but she really did "Make a Difference." I went on a Self - Management Leadership Course run by The Brahma Kumaris Spiritual University. It was based at The Global Retreat Centre at Oxford. We were given time out to take stock of our lives and see where we were at. We thought about the next stage of our life and what title we would give the next chapter of our life. The idea of "Making a Difference" tumbled into my mind and the idea cropped up yet again that I should write a book. This seed of an idea has been eating away at me since the day she died. What a legacy to leave for my family. If Cooper and Polly have the opportunity to read about the way my mind works and the way I came to terms with the situation then they may benefit. Every other person that reads the book will be a bonus. It will mean that Katie really did "Make a Difference."

That weekend tears flowed. Healing tears, that like a river, take you somewhere. Weeping creates water around the boat, allowing it to float. Who knows where your little boat, or tender will take you. Tears make you tender, a bit like tenderizing a steak, I guess. Tears lift the boat out of the rocks, off dry land and carry it to some place new. Maybe some place better. Tears are lenses through which we may be able to gain an alternative vision. They say that what you are seeking is also seeking you. If you sit or lie still, it will seek you out. It has been waiting for you for a long time. Just relax and see what happens.

Imagine the body informs the soul and helps it to adapt to mundane life. Life wasn't mundane after Katie but, for a while, it just wasn't worth living. With ink the soul can write on the blank page of our lives. As I see it, the body is the rocket launcher. In its nose capsule the soul looks out of the window into the mysterious starry light and is dazzled. Was Katie too dazzled? Was she called away so soon because she was drawn to the bright light. Her soul was dazzled and she left too soon. She played with the cord and the curtains closed around her. Maybe depriving a mother of her child is greater than depriving a child of her mother. I don't know, I have only experienced one side of the equation.

This probably sounds weird and you may think this is mad and decide to stop reading. It isn't crazy and I haven't been drinking. This is the place I go when I meditate. I go to the little room behind my eyes and this is the camera to the world. They say that your eyes are the windows to your soul. Light forms an image on "your mind's eye" and you can travel anywhere in the world. Strangely enough, I have never travelled to meet Katie. Instead meditation allows me to clear my head. My mind is like muddy waters. During quiet time things are allowed to settle. What to do and what not to do is obvious and clear. It makes it easier to decide what to say and what not to say. Sometimes it is just perfect to say nothing at all.

You can meditate anywhere. You simply go within and focus on your breathing. Slow your thoughts and begin to relax. Let go. Relax your whole body from the tip of your toes to the top of your head. Tune into the rhythm within and "chillax!" It is like giving your whole body a holiday by just packing your thoughts away for you to fly away to your very own destination. We use only a small percentage of our brain. I guess our brain is like an iceberg and we usually use only the tip of our iceberg.

No amount of deep breathing and meditating
Can change your past
But
You can change tomorrow
By your thoughts and actions today.

The Rose

"Dear rose without a thorn
The bud's babe unborn
First streak of a new morn."

(Robert Browning)

I hadn't heard or read these lines when Katie was born-died, but the rose is the symbol that comes to mind when I think of her.

The chaplin at The University Hospital of Wales was brilliant. He spent time talking to Ivor and I during labour. He was there to smile, support and speak with our own vicar. Ivor and I had recently been to confirmation classes with "Nic the Vic" – our friendly way of referring to him. Although the chaplin was on hand Nicholas drove into Cardiff to baptise Katie at three in the morning. He knew us well enough to know what we needed.

For the Baptism I sat up in bed and found strength from somewhere. Do you know the feeling when you cannot sing because there is a lump the size of a melon in your throat? Ivor couldn't say the words in the service but he held Katie and looked in wonder and disbelief. I could sing purely because when I became aware that baby Katie had stopped moving inside me, it was real for me. It was not real for Ivor until she was born and he held her in his arms. She was so perfect, so still and totally silent. I often wonder whether she wanted to leave us. I guess she didn't have a choice.

When I read Katie's entry in the Book of Remembrance for Babies Loved and Lost at The University Hospital of Wales it reminds me to slow down and take time to smell the roses. The entry reads:

"Our rose sent to bud on earth and bloom in heaven.
Another angel for God's garden."

I often wonder why God needed my little angel in particular. Surely, if God is so clever why couldn't He or She have just made a new one? She was new and although she had been around no time at all, she has friends and family in heaven. I have friends on earth that kept me sane at such a sad time. The whole episode made we question God and the way He or She works. In the pattern of life not every thread can be golden. Only a mixture of dark and light shades will give us any chance of seeing the bigger picture:

"My life is but a weaving between my Lord and me;
I cannot choose the colours He worketh steadily.
Oftentimes He weaveth sorrow and I in foolish pride,
Forget that He sees the upper, and I the underside.
Not till the loom is silent and the shuttles cease to fly.
Shall God unroll the canvas and explain the reason why
The dark threads are needed in the weaver's skilful
hand
As the threads of gold and silver in the pattern He has
planned."

By
(Benjamin Malachi Franklin)

We don't know the whole picture. When things go

wrong we can't always see the reason why and see how it fits in with the whole scheme of things. When you look back over your life I think that it starts to make more sense. I believe that at the very end of our life everything will become crystal clear. Although we may understand our life if we start at the end and look backwards you must live your life forwards. Sometimes it is important to pause and other times fast- forward is the only way through. It is important to remember that everybody dies but not everybody lives. If you live today and every day as if it were your last day on earth, then you will be living life in the fast lane.

As soon as I see a rose I think of Katie. It is like an automatic reflex in the same way your mouth waters when you think of your favourite food. I wish I had heard the song entitled "The Rose" before Katie's funeral because I would have loved for it to have been included. All Things Bright and Beautiful and Gentle Jesus Meek and Mild were just perfect. Yes... we chose two children's hymns and neither Ivor or I could sing. In fact just thinking of the words "look upon this little child" brings tears to my eyes. Whenever I hear them, in whatever the context, I really have to brace myself to be able to sing. "The Rose, " and the final lines in particular have a similar affect.

> "...Just remember in the winter
> Far beneath the bitter snows
> For the need love is sown.
> Lies the seed that with the sun's love
> In the spring becomes the rose."

"The Rose" is featured in the film of the same name in which it was performed by Bette Midler. It has been performed by others. Every word on every line means something to me. Katie is the "tender weed" but, she didn't drown, she managed to get tangled in the cord. She tied herself up in knots that meant she wouldn't survive. Souls within the family were left "to bleed" or grieve. To make it all worthwhile there had to be another Rose or Polly, in our case. There was "an endless aching need," not to replace Katie because you can't do that but, I desperately wanted to walk out of the hospital with a screaming baby in my arms. I need to re-run the film with a different ending – a happy ending. Do you remember the "French Lieutenant's Woman?" The film nicely combines history and the modern day and there are two different endings. I may be a romantic but I wanted a happy ending. When we watched the film in the cinema Ivor fell asleep. Bearing in mind the ending I want there is little chance of a good night's sleep. We have to remember that there are no straight lines in nature. Everything is cyclical and everything happens in its own time. There is an incubation period for everything – ideas as well as babies. Nobody becomes an immediate success overnight, it takes careful planning, picturing and sheer grit. Ultimately, winter is over and spring time arrives. YES!

> "Like the seed that is the sun's love
> In the spring becomes the rose."

Spring always follows winter, and out of struggle comes new growth. Nothing lasts forever and the whole of life is a cycle. What is good will go bad and what is bad will change. Trust that difficulties will be resolved and your dreams can be realised. We don't always get the outcome we want and our expectations are not always met, but what we do get always shows it to be for the best in the long run. When you order food in a restaurant you don't go to the kitchen to check that it is being cooked. You trust that it will arrive at your table and it does, at some point. Assume that your dreams are already in the cosmic kitchen and be ready when they put in an appearance. Also it is important to make sure you order what you really want as your order may not be quite as you imagined.

I am into patchwork. My uncle thinks that I am crazy to cut up a perfectly good piece of fabric only to sew it back together again! Life is a great big patchwork quilt. There are dark patches next to light ones. When the shadows fade and the sun comes shining through it reminds me of a fairy tale. Good invariably triumphs over evil and Cinderella goes to the ball. Spring follows winter.

Watching the service at St Paul's Cathedral on the first anniversary of the Twin Towers disaster. I feel the familiar churning feeling in my stomach as I see the candles lit in remembrance. I think of the candles lit at the University Hospital of Wales, one for each baby loved and lost. Every Easter Sunday there is a service at the University Hospital of Wales. My mum and I attend the service and when Cooper asked to come I thought he was old enough to deal with it. My mum and I thought that we had misjudged the situation when Cooper started to cry. After a cuddle he confessed that he was afraid the building would burn down. Seeing the world through the eyes of a child is so different and it really sheds light on the situation.

Tears roll down my cheeks as the tiny white rose petals float to rest on the cathedral floor. Three thousand petals to remember the three thousand people who lost their lives that dreadful September day. As friends and family decide to gather a petal to keep to remember their loved ones I think how wonderful to be able to take something home as a keepsake. For me the white petal is both a symbol of winter and spring.

White for purity and the winter snow. The petal, a beautiful part of the rose that flowers in the spring. When you are grieving you think that the sun will never shine and warm your face again but, spring always follows winter.

My favourite crystal is rose quartz. The clear, almost translucent pale pink stone of gentle healing is known as the children's stone. It is used to soothe away childhood ills and sorrows. It promotes family love and friendship, brings peace, self- forgiveness and is said to increase confidence. I regularly sleep with a rose quartz under my pillow. Most mornings Cooper and Polly climb into "the big bed" for a cuddle. On one particular morning I was quite stressed because I was attending a job interview and I really wanted the job. My crystal had gone walk about during the night and Cooper happened to lie on it. "What on earth is this?"He shouts. "Mum why have you got a stone in bed with you?"He is pretty astute as he knows that the crystal couldn't possibly be his dad's. I explain what it is and why it was beneath my pillow. Before we get up I ask Cooper if he has any words of wisdom for my interview. He said "if I were you Mum, I wouldn't tell them that you sleep with a stone under your pillow that you hold and talk to!" He makes me sound totally mad. By the way, I landed the job and bought myself a bunch of baby pink roses to celebrate my success in style.

The Butterfly

"Don't weep at my grave,
For I am not there.
I've a date with a butterfly
To dance in the air.
I'll be singing in the sunshine,
Wild and free,
Playing tag with the wind
While I'm waiting for thee.
What the caterpillar calls the end of the world,
The master calls a
butterfly."

(By Richard Bach)

Does your heart go out to the caterpillar? It is the end of the world as the caterpillar knows it, but we know that the butterfly is about to put in an appearance. If only we had such information in all aspects of our life.

Do you know the story of the very hungry caterpillar? He ate for a week. He ate so much that he was at bursting point. One week later he exploded into a butterfly. I was a hungry caterpillar. Hungry for work and promotion. Hungry to study as I saw this as a means to an end – a means to get the promotion I wanted. The butterfly didn't land the minute Katie was born. It took time. The wings needed time to dry off and to take a well – earned rest. The butterfly landed on the most beautiful rose imaginable before taking flight. I stayed at home for seven years, resting before taking up real, paid work again. I always thought it was a lot of nonsense when people talk about the seven year itch, but this is how long I took to feel I was ready to face the world of work again. I was determined to find the right work for me. It had to be meaningful work that would make a difference.

The caterpillar and the butterfly both have the same soul, but the butterfly is on an entirely different plane. This is how different I feel. I am nothing like the person I used to be. Have you seen a diamond in the rough before it is polished? After polishing it is the same diamond but it looks entirely different. A chunk of rose quartz looks different if it is polished. The rough edges have been forcefully removed and the result is a priceless gem. I am not saying that I am a priceless gem but I have been called "Priceless" and I am a new version of my former self.

Iron becomes steel when it has been through the fire. The finished product may not look bigger, but it is stronger. When you live through any kind of trauma it inevitably makes you stronger in the end. It takes time because everything happens in its own time not in your time. When the student is ready the teacher appears and you too can become a butterfly.

The butterfly, like the rose keeps cropping up in my life. At swimming they taught Polly to wave or "wriggle" in the water with her knees and feet together. Wrapping the towel around her after the lesson I said "that was a great butterfly, Polly!" She looks at me as if I have flipped and said "Mum, butterflies don't swim, that was a dolphin!" Absolutely nothing stays the same. The stroke may be the same but that is as far as it goes. The name is now more meaningful. You can become free and fly like a butterfly or swim with the dolphins. Just make time to smell the roses as you journey through the fast, hectic, high- pressured world we live in.

Like the traveller in the story, it is good to see old places with new eyes. The traveller asks the old man at the side of the road what the villagers in the settlement ahead are like. The old man asks the traveller how he found the people in the village he had just left. "I found them all friendly and most helpful" replied the traveller. "Then you will find them much the same in the village ahead" replied the old man. The moral of the story is that people tend to treat you as they find you. Hence the villagers at both locations will treat the traveller with kindness.

It is important to let go of bad experiences and learn from them. This proves that they had a purpose. You will meet good and bad people in your life. The ones you like may be your friends. Remember the good people and experiences and make them your friends. Much of the pain and frustration we experience is the result of resistance to that which is not only out of our control, but also what we feel is unfair or should not happen to us. If we can replace this resistance with acceptance, stop judging and start learning from the unpredictable events of our life, we begin to discover another key to happiness.

Things may change in a split second. Katie changed our lives in an instant and forever. Whatever had we done wrong as a family? Why us? Why this? It took years for it to become crystal clear. On a meditation course the tutor said that "Katie was stillborn." Her life had a purpose because she changed my attitude and my life forever. I now aim to live my life in the sunshine. I savour every experience life throws at me, both good and bad. Life may be a roller coaster but it is important to enjoy the ride.

Why in the midst of laughing with Polly am I thinking of Katie? There are tears in my eyes as I think that Katie will never learn to sail, go horse riding or play the drums. The "first everything" is always going to be hard. The first time it snowed after Katie died, I remember saying to my mum "Katie hasn't seen snow." My mum is a wise old owl because her reply came quickly "How do you know?" Her reply speaks volumes. While I am sitting laughing and crying at the same time just as if I am practicing some kind of mantra, Katie may be playing her own little drum kit in the sky. Polly's first trip out meant walking down a road called "Tough Love." I loved spending time with Polly but it was tough because I was so aware that there was no first trip out with Katie. No first day at nursery and no school uniform to purchase. Her feet were never measured to buy her shoes. I don't even have an empty shoe box let alone a pair of shoes. I wonder if these thoughts will ever end. Time tells me that they do not stop but they reduce and they reduce. Like the level of water in a reservoir during a period of drought. Polly passing her driving test and the arrival of her first car still hit home. If Polly ever marries I guess I will pretend that Katie is Matron of Honour so everybody is included in the celebrations. I savour Polly, I drink her in and we have adjacent changing rooms in our quest for clothes. We both love shoes and as we are both a size four we sometimes share. I wonder what size shoe Katie wears right now. When she was born I remember thinking her feet and her hands were big. I am so glad we took the risk of another pregnancy. I might never have known the joy of cuddling my screaming baby girl. We can never stop thinking but we can watch our thoughts and make sure that they are positive. Remember, we are what we think so we may as well be positive.

S.C.B.U.

At the special care baby unit at The University Hospital of Wales, I peered through the window and saw Polly in a tiny incubator because she had a "snuffly" nose and they popped a tiny tube into her tummy to make things easier. I am looking at a room full of baby fighters. It is a pity that Katie didn't have a chance to put up a fight.

Some of the babies were one day old or even younger. Each one beginning a race with the same opportunity to win. I wonder what will make the difference ten, twenty or thirty years from now. Why may one be a contributor and one a hindrance to society? Will one be happy and content through life, while another lives in the shadows? Polly, lying there so quiet, will she make a difference in the world and be a kind, caring soul? Without taking a breath, her sister, Katie made a difference. We each have an equal start – what makes the difference?

I think that children learn from what they hear, see, feel, touch and are touched by. They taste adult's actions. They learn just as much from what is unsaid as the spoken word.

Children Learn What They Live
If a child lives with criticism
He learns to condemn
If a child lives with hostility
He learns to fight
If a child lives with ridicule
He learns to be shy
If a child lives with shame
He learns to have guilt
If a child lives with tolerance
He learns to be patient
If a child lives with encouragement
He learns to have confidence
If a child lives with praise
He learns to appreciate
If a child lives with fairness
He learns justice
If a child lives with approval
He learns to like himself
If a child lives with acceptance and friendship
He learns to find love in the world.

By
(Dorothy Law Nolte PhD)

Some of the babies in the special baby care unit may go on and make a difference in the world. I always say to Cooper and Polly "You can do anything you want in your life, as long as it is good and legal." I don't want them to think that they can rob a bank, but I want them to have confidence in their ability and to take responsibility for their own life. This is similar to the message Billy Joel's Mum gave to her son. Her message was "Don't go changing." Imagine her surprise when Billy Joel echoed these words back to her in his Grammy award winning song – "Don't go changing – I love you just the way you are." The key is to be you. Visualise the outcome you want and go for it. If life is good and the sun shines for you it is easier but you can survive and even thrive with the right state of mind. When life throws you a lemon don't screw up your face – go for the juicer and make lemonade. You could even add a couple of shots of vodka for good measure. As a child were you ever given a Christmas present that required batteries and there were none there? In the first instance it says a lot about the person giving the present but, it also says a lot about the way most of us lead our lives. Like the toy, ready for action but, we don't have the batteries. We've lost our bottle, if we ever had it. Some of the babies in the special baby care unit will dig deep in a pocket and find batteries somewhere. Tell me… Are your batteries running low? Are you running on empty? How can you change things for the better? It wouldn't be unusual to feel low during a stay in prison. A lad in a prison in the centre of a desert looks out and he can either see mud or stars. Do you see stars or scars? Remember, human spirit can triumph over seemingly insurmountable odds.

In Jonathan Livingston Seagull, Jonathan believes that he is a special seagull. He knows that he is different and plans to make a difference. He doesn't follow the crowd. When he tries to behave like the other gulls he thought it all so pointless. Jonathan's secret is that he keeps on keeping on and he will not accept anything less.

"Why, Jon, why; his mother asked
Why is it so hard to be like the rest of the flock, Jon?"

(Jonathan Livingstone Seagull by Richard Bach.)

Do you believe that you are unique and special? In

the whole of history there has never been anyone like you before. You have a contribution to make to your world that no-one else can make. When I work with a group of students I believe that I am the right person to make them feel special. I believe that God has placed me there to make a difference in their lives.

Do you believe that you can do anything you want in life? Rather than thinking that "seeing is believing" it is important to realize that "believing is seeing." Whenever I need that extra bit of faith I sing the song in my mind….. "I Believe I can fly, I believe I can touch the sky….etc." Why shouldn't we stand out from the crowd?

We have all copied someone else at some point in our lives. Do you remember buying that expensive outfit that looked great on your mate but it just didn't suit you? Have you gone to a restaurant that someone else thought was the best thing since sliced bread only to find that it wasn't your cup of tea. This happens because we are all unique and we all like different things. Always be yourself in life. Copying others doesn't work. By all means make a note of someone's good points and model your behaviour on them but don't be a copycat.

I am aiming to become "the best me that I can be," since losing Katie. The caterpillar becomes a butterfly and I try to sharpen my colours and serve more flowers each and every day. Post Katie, post-mortem, post depression I really feel that I am true to myself, most of the time. I am human and sometimes I still try too hard to please others. I sometimes feel sorry for myself but I haven't suffered with a bout of depression for many years. More often I see the bigger picture and sometimes I even manage to keep things in perspective. Katie taught me to please myself and do what is right for me and my family.

Success and failure are on the same road. Success is just a bit further on. It's not your action but your reaction that determines your degree of success. It is important to programme your life for success. Life is a self- fulfilling prophecy and in life you get what you expect to happen. Don't be surprised when your way of thinking rubs off on your family. Cooper is into golf so he is familiar with the idea of "giving it your best shot!" He practices, he pictures the ball disappearing down the hole and he knows that the only place success comes before work is in the dictionary.

Without a doubt Katie has affected many lives far and wide. Robert Frost, in "The Road Not Taken" sums this up rather nicely. Do you take the easy option or do you make life difficult for yourself? I rarely take the easy option. I usually take the "road less travelled by, and that made all the difference."

I never take the easy option in life. Why have a part-time job when you can run your own business. Why have a regular income when you can ride the financial roller coaster and have fun with the family. Katie has taught me to live life in the fast lane with the throttle to the floor Maybe the road less travelled, with fewer cars on the highway, is a safer bet.

"Merci"

We are like nomads. Each summer and most weekends we load the Discovery or "Disco" as we call it. We pack the touring caravan and we finally balance Ivor's sailing boat on the Disco roof rack and off we go. Cooper in search of fish, Ivor and Polly to sail and I just potter about in between running circles around all of them. It was while we were at a caravan park, sipping wine in the rain that the rose bloomed again. We had a smashing family for neighbours and their three children played with our two children. Us Mums talked as if we were old friends meeting up. I must have told her about my desire to write a book. We exchanged views on books we found inspiring and I lent her my copy of "Jonathan Livingston Seagull" by Bach. In return she lent me her copy of "The Little Prince by Antoine De Saint Exupery."

The author of The Little Price was a pilot and in the book the narrator has crash landed in the Sahara desert in 1935 and very nearly died of thirst. From his devastating experience of the loneliness came "The Little Prince." The book is a joyous look at how crazy adults are. He describes a businessman whom is so busy counting the stars he believes he "owns" that he is unable to appreciate a single one of them. There is a train switch operator who routes and re-routes express trains full of people who do not know where they are going or why they are going there. Only the children enjoy the trip, their noses pressed against the windows. There is a merchant selling pills designed to quench thirst so that one may "save" 53 minutes. "As for me," says the Little Prince to the airman "if I had 53 minutes to spend as I liked I should walk at my leisure towards a spring of fresh water."

When I teach time management I sometimes ask the students what they would do if they had 53 minutes to spare. Often they share clever examples of ways to save time but why do we usually try to fill our free time with even more things? Why can't we just be? After all we are "human beings" not "human doings."

Surprise, surprise the Little Prince looks after a rose. She was "a coquettish creature." She showed herself one morning as a huge, green bud....

"But the little flower was not satisfied to complete the preparations for her beauty in the shelter of her green chamber. She chose her colours with the greatest of care. She dressed herself slowly She adjusted her petals one by one. She did not want to go out into the world all rumpled, like the field poppies. It was only in the full radiance of her beauty that she wished to appear." The little Prince looked after the rose and kept her safe from draughts. She was difficult, vain and demanding – a bit like me on a bad hair day! She set The Little Prince thinking and put him in a state of analysis paralysis and beats himself up, as we all do.

"The fact is that I did not know how to understand anything! I ought to have judged her by her deeds and not by words. She cast her fragrance and radiance over me. I ought never to have run away from her... I ought to have guessed all the affection that lay behind the poor little stratagems. Flowers are inconsistent! But I was too young to know how to love her..." The Little Prince is hard on himself and, at times, we are all hard on ourselves. If we talked to our friends the way we talk to our selves I wonder how many friends would stick around?

People, like roses, don't always say what they mean. Sometimes, when someone has died we feel that we have to say something; even it is the wrong thing. Sometimes actions speak louder than words and a touch on the arm or a knowing glance and smile can speak volumes. I found this far kinder after Katie's death than the people who felt they needed to give you the benefit of their advice. Just as the fragrance of the rose was far kinder to The Little Prince than her harsh words, just being there for someone is far better and is often the greatest comfort at times of sorrow.

I remember feeling hurt when people crossed to the other side of the road because they didn't know what to say to me. Most hurtful were the people who said something to fill the silence and cover their embarrassment without thinking first. When I was pregnant with Polly I remember one lady saying to me "You look after yourself this time." Just as if I didn't look after myself when I was pregnant with Katie. It gets worse as when Polly was born some people thought they were helping when they said "Well, at least you have a little girl now. It's as if they thought that someone had waved a magic wand, the past was forgotten and life was instantly brilliant. Prince Charming (in the guise of Polly) arrives and her warmth and the touch of her velvet skin awake me from my trance and we live happily ever after. Life isn't like that because life isn't a fairy story and we cannot always have a happy ending. I guess well wishers thought they were being helpful but, how can one child replace another? Nobody can replace the child that you have lost and nothing can take the pain away, in an instant. Unless you have experienced losing a child or grand – child maybe it just cannot be understood. I guess it is like trying to describe a place you haven't visited. Not easy to do with feeling. Why is it then that some people manage to say and do just the right things, just at the right time?

We have been to France many times and I love the feel of the place. It was on a French campsite that Cooper swerved to avoid a child and his jacket became caught in the wheel on his bike. In a heap, bleeding and crying, several people walked straight past and left him in the dust. One kind man half carried him back to our caravan. Cooper explained what happened and the story of the Good Samaritan tumbled into my mind. It was only when Cooper's knee had been stitched that I was calm enough to wonder why there are butterflies in my stomach. During many bouts of depression I have learned to deal with this feeling. To breathe the feeling away and to stay in control. The secret is to get the butterflies to fly in formation and to work for you instead of against you. The butterflies are settling and I am back at the University Hospital of Wales. Polly is five days old and even after a caesarean I insisted on going to the church for morning service. Ivor pushed me there in a wheelchair and Polly was in my arms, "on the latch" as Cooper used to call it. The Chaplin, whom had helped us through the night waiting for Katie's arrival, walked down the aisle. He took time to look down at Polly. I will never forget his words "What a beautiful baby!" It's a good job we didn't have twins because he might well have said "What a beautiful pair!" To laugh would have been especially painful and probably not appropriate. The only time I have ever had boobs is when I am breast feeding so it would have been a compliment and just the thought of the situation still brings a smile to my face and as I picture the sparkle in the Chaplin's eyes.

The reading in the service was "The Good Samaritan" and I thought of Connie, my personal "Good Samaritan" who helped me through every hospital visit when I was pregnant with Polly. Funnily enough Connie bought Cooper a book to celebrate Polly's baptism. The book has the very same title. I must have told Connie about my hospital stay when Polly was born. She truly listened to me. She understood me. She gave Cooper the perfect gift to remember Polly's safe arrival and her Baptism. Thank-you Connie.

I guess I wanted to swell the numbers at the church service to say thank – you to the Chaplin for his support. I also wanted to say thank you to God for the privilege of looking after Polly. He had other plans for Katie but, I thank God that Ivor and I were entrusted to look after Polly. I often wonder why I did not feel angry with God. We were both hurting. I talked non - stop about it and Ivor said very little at all. I guess men and women deal with things differently. Our experiences were different and our perception of the situation was light years apart. If anything, my experience with Katie had strengthened my faith. I know that things might not turn out as you expect or want but that things can turn out well. Life is a test. Sometimes the test is difficult. At times it may even feel that we are given the test to sit without first having the lesson. I'm a trainer and I know that the seed of the lesson sits in a lesson plan. With faith you can pass "Go," claim £200 and live happily ever after. How lucky am I to have Cooper, Polly and the cherished memories of baby Katie's short stay to ensure I keep this game of life in perspective. I must not forget Tom. My quest for a family started with a miscarriage and I was afraid that I might never be a mother. Although I never really knew what sex the baby would have been I always knew that he was my little boy. I never held him so it has never felt real. Instead it is surreal.

I could never go on to list everyone I need to say thank you to. Not just the man in the camp site in France, the staff at The University Hospital of Wales, Eglwys Bach Surgery at Pontypridd, friends, family and total strangers who listened when I needed to talk. I remember visiting the Registry office to register Katie's birth and death. The lady was brilliant at her job. She made an entry on the credit side to include a new arrival, and an entry on the debit side to balance the books. She was kind and made no attempt to rush me through the door. We talked about Cooper and life in general. She eased my nightmare although it still felt like a pointless, waste of time. Cooper was a toddler and too young to understand, but my little boy kept me sane while awaiting Polly's arrival. How lucky am I? An attitude of gratitude is essential. "Thank you Ivor for never giving up on me back there at such a sad time when I was at my lowest ebb." I am now in danger of drowning my lap top with my tears so it is time to take a break and stop typing.

Last Respects

After carrying out the post mortem The University Hospital of Wales would have arranged to bury Katie at the baby cemetery at Thornhill, Cardiff.

We wanted a family plot.
We wanted a cremation.

We wanted only family flowers and donations to The Foundation for the study of Infant Deaths (FSID).

We organised what we wanted.

I can picture Ivor and I sitting in the funeral director's office, heads bowed, both studying our shoes. The carpet was pale and the curtains were drawn. Pale and drawn like our tired faces. He discussed the weight of the ashes following the cremation and whether there would be sufficient for burial. Oh my God this is unreal. It felt a little more real when we discussed what Katie would wear. Let's keep it plain and simple. Let her stay in her white baby-grow the one with the white satin collar. The hospital already handled her too much so please let her rest peacefully.

Katie was brought back to the family home on the eve of 20th September 1993 ready for the funeral the next day. A little white coffin the size of a shoe box and trimmed with pale pink lace. It is ironic that she would never have a pair of shoes, not even the soft, fabric ones that babies first wear. I was upstairs settling Cooper when the undertaker arrived. I read an extra story and didn't want to leave him. I was scared to go and hug Katie. The last hug and the last kiss. How sad that this will have to last a lifetime. The hospital post-mortem had broken her. They had handled her more than I had and I'm supposed to be her mum. Unlike Humpty Dumpty, nothing could put my little angel back together again.

We put a couple of things inside her coffin with her. A photograph of Ivor, Cooper and me, so she would know her immediate family. When Polly reads this I know she will ask "What about me – why aren't I in the photograph?" We didn't have a photograph or even a scan of you at that stage, as you weren't even conceived until a month later. My parting thoughts to God were "If you can do a better job of looking after Katie than us you had better do a good job of it and, I haven't finished yet, watch she doesn't catch cold and make sure her shoes fit properly. I couldn't handle passing the job of raising Katie over to God without adding my pennyworth.

Uncle Glyn, my dad's brother, and one of my colleagues helped "Nic the Vic" through the service at my parents' house. Uncle Glyn read the poem "A Child Loaned" by Edgar A. Guest.

"I'll lend you for a little time
A child of Mine," He said,
"For you to love the while she lives,
And mourn for when she's dead.
It may be six or seven years
Or twenty- two or three,

45

But will you till I call her back,
Take care of her for Me?
She'll bring her charms to gladden you,
And should her stay be brief,
You'll have her lovely memories
As solace for your grief."

There are three verses and Uncle Glyn read the first one. I was sandwiched on the sofa between Ivor and my Mum. I didn't take my eyes off the tiny coffin sitting in front of me. We didn't have six or seven years with Katie. We didn't have six or seven minutes or six or seven breaths. She was never ill and I had no warning of what was to come. Her time in God's waiting room, waiting to die was limited to her time inside me. One minute Katie and I were together, like a couple, joined as one and then I was single. No longer pregnant. No longer carrying baby Katie. My body was my own. My body was single once more. What, was God thinking? Why would I carry baby Katie to full term for God to take her back straight away? He must have had his reasons and all I can say is that they had better be worthy of His or Her actions.

I can't even recall who read the one final quotation from The Little Prince by Antoine de Saint- Exupery. The words really touched the spot because they made me feel as if Katie was speaking them herself. She was speaking just to me and she was telling me that she was going to be fine. She tells me where she would be living – just like passing your new address to friends and family when you move house. I guess Katie was relocating. The funeral was one, big, fancy removal van and my help with her move was strictly limited.

"In one of the stars, I shall be living.
In one of them, I shall be laughing.

46

And so it will be as if the stars are laughing
When you look at the sky at night."

(The Little Prince, Antoine de Saint-Exupery)

We hadn't decided who would carry Katie to the car, but Ivor took responsibility and perched her on the back seat of the limousine between us. I look at her coffin and wish I could look inside just one last time. I can't. I'm not allowed. I don't see a "No Entry" label but, I just have to picture Katie twinkling like a bright shiny star within her tiny removal van heading for her home in the sky.

When we arrived at the crematorium I remember waving and smiling at the crowds. I was acting more like a film star at her gala performance than a Mum arriving at her daughter's funeral. I was there but I wasn't there. I couldn't take in the detail and I was some place far away. I couldn't deal with the situation and didn't want to deal with it. I felt numb and as we walked into the church. My legs were propelling me forwards but, at the same time I didn't feel as if I was moving. Moving, but not moving. Present but this is no gift. We have all walked on air when we feel full of joy. I was walking on air with a head full of cotton wool while feeling physically sick and I was anything but full of joy. The last time I felt sick it was morning sickness. I want to curl up and sleep peacefully next to baby Katie but Cooper needs me and I have to be strong for him.

"I am the resurrection and the light..."

Everything after that was a blur. Ivor and I couldn't sing. My mouth was dry and I felt sick. I couldn't breathe and I wanted to escape and yet I remained fixed to the spot. When the curtains closed I realise that I was forgetting to breathe. Where was the car? How will I stand and speak to these people. I have to thank the people for attending. I owe it to them, to Katie and myself. I look, I cry and I lean on Ivor in the same way that I have done so many times throughout our life together. We focus on each other as we have peace of mind that Cooper is being cared for.

FSID was and still is close to my heart. Sarah, representing FSID, a lovely, lovely lady came to visit me at home. She kept me sane and helped with the simple day to day tasks I suddenly found so difficult. She befriended me at so many levels. Donations in lieu of flowers were destined to the coffers of FSID to help other families through their hurt and grief. We did the right thing with the flowers. The coffin stood so small and too many flowers would have smothered baby Katie. She is free from the troubles and stresses of this world. FSID has been renamed The Lullaby Trust. I just love the name, what the charity does and what it stands for.

Cooper was a toddler when Katie died. We were prepared at home for the new baby- well sort of, if you call living in a caravan while we built a house being prepared! We couldn't have the funeral from the building site and the family home was fitting. Cooper went to nursery school as usual. Maybe it wasn't the right decision for Cooper but I couldn't have coped with a two year old at the funeral. A good friend of mine picked Cooper up from nursery and took him back to her home. I know they had a picnic and played with her son's rabbit. The rabbit was called Lucky and it might have been lucky for Cooper that he was able to play with and cuddle the rabbit. I felt trapped at the funeral. Katie was cremated. Imagine him asking about the curtain and the little white box disappearing. I remember Cooper moving the curtain in a puppet show to see what was going on behind the scenes. It was a party and the puppet show was the entertainment. The colour drained from the entertainers face when I gave her the good news that she was at Cooper's party in a couple of weeks. Anyway I just couldn't have coped. At the time he said very little, but when I went into hospital to have Polly, he asked "Are you bringing this one home?" So matter of fact and as if I just couldn't be bothered to bring Katie home.

I know we didn't give Cooper the chance to say goodbye and this may seem selfish but I could just about keep myself together. I was beginning to feel like the boiled frog Charles Handy refers to. His theory is that the frog is adaptable and if you put a frog in a pan of cold water and gently heat it the frog gradually gets used to the temperature and doesn't jump out. The church felt like a big plastic bag draped around me and I felt like the frog with the temperature rising just like a boil in the bag convenience meal. There was nothing convenient about the situation. When you get married you have a rehearsal. There was no rehearsal before Katie's funeral and I was slowly reaching boiling point – my very own melt down. The first time I was thrown into boiling water was at the hospital when they turned the screen away and told me there was no heart beat. The second time was at the funeral. I felt as if I was floating, sinking and slipping under water all at the same time.

There, in front of me, on the stall in the French market sat a family of wooden frogs. Maybe it was the strange croaking sound that drew me to the stall. Each frog had a piece of wood in its mouth which could be removed and rubbed across the frog's back to make the croaking sound. Sounds a bit weird, I know, but quite an authentic sound. Each frog had been hollowed out.

They had a zig- zag shape carved down the centre of their back. We chose to purchase the grandmother size. What would we call her? "Stegathorus, Handy..." It doesn't say made in Taiwan or China or whatever on her "derriere" so, we'll settle for Katie. As a mark of respect, I decided to pass on the idea of tasting frog's legs and leave this experience for another time.

I stood at the market stall with a tear in my eye. Again I have a tear in my eye as I look at the grandmother frog perched on her shelf. Regularly I find a tiny white feather in the most unusual places. My eyes light up at the sight of a feather left by an angel. Not any old angel, our angel – little Katie Price. A feather is sitting close to the frog. Katie approves. If I was making a collage I would probably make the clouds out of cotton wool or feathers. Clouds look like bundles of white feathers. If you look close you see pictures and faces in the clouds. Real faces of people, and animals of all shapes and sizes. Take a look and look closer and make a mental note of what you see. As I look skyward I wonder if I will see Katie's face in the clouds.

I don't remember if the sky was cloudy on the day of Katie's funeral. I spent so long studying my shoes, I just don't know. About a month after her funeral I attended another funeral in the same church and at the same cemetery. The funeral wasn't in memory of a close family member but I cried like a baby. My mum understood. In my mind I was back as Katie's funeral once more and it seemed more painful the second time around. Maybe Katie's funeral was a rehearsal after all. At the funeral the Priest offered a story of consolation. He described a congregation of people on the shore, sadly waving goodbye to a ship. It diminishes in size until only the tip of the mast is visible. When that too vanishes, the onlookers murmur, "she's gone." At that very instant, however, somewhere far away, another group of people are scanning the horizon, and seeing the tip of the mast appear, they exclaim "She's come!"

I guess the story really hit home because it is about boats and water, friends coming and going and a loved one moving to pastures new. We all move on to new ventures and meet new people. The cruel thing is that Katie didn't get a chance in this world. She disappeared over the horizon much too soon. The order is wrong. Your children should not die before you. Katie wasn't born prematurely but her departure certainly was premature.

A couple of days later, when Katie's ashes were cool a small group of us attended the cemetery for the committal. I throw the palest pink rose onto the fresh earth. I look up at the cloudy sky. The clouds are moving quickly and the sun isn't shining. The only positive thought I muster before we leave is the fact that she is on the very edge of the cemetery. Beyond the boundary fence children play in the street. It is so unfair that she will never play here on earth. The party start to move towards the car. I am rooted to the spot and I stare at the earth. I think of the mole hills that sometimes appear in my Dad's otherwise perfect lawn and I want the earth to move in front of my eyes. Moles move. Ash is silent and still. I am standing still and still staring as Ivor gently holds my hand and encourages me to walk away. I stand outside the car and I look at Katie's spot. I get in the car and with my nose pressed to the glass I keep looking. I stare and the glass steams up. I start to cry as this is yet another thing that Katie will not do. On the glass I draw a tiny heart and I blow her a kiss. To bridge the gap I imagine she blows us a kiss. I really don't want to leave her but Ivor drives slowly out through the gates into nothingness.

The Swallows Nest

When you have a miscarriage there is no funeral to mark the end of a life. When we got married neither of us were in a rush to have children. In fact, I don't remember even discussing it and we focus on renovating our first home. We bought a perfectly okay, but tastelessly decorated semi- detached house. Polly used to call them "attached houses" and this seems much more sensible. The Little Prince is right, we can learn so much from our children.

The entrance hall was painted dark brown. The dining room had mustard coloured skirting boards which had been painted without covering the carpet so the room looked as if it had double yellows. I guess this fitted in with the fast pace of our lives. There is no time to delay over food today just about sums it up.

When we started pulling down the walls to build an extension we found some kind of straw insulation. When I take Polly for her horse riding lesson, every time I see the straw in the stables, I think about how I studied for the finals of my degree in my very own "attached" stable. I could have completed the course in three years, but why do this when you can take five years part time, work full time and re- build your first home? I never take the easy option in life. Are you harder on yourself than you would be on your own worst enemy? Why do we treat ourselves so badly?

Don't we deserve an easy ride at least now and again?

Five years later, Ivor designed a house for his mate and it got us thinking. Why don't we build our own house? We bought a couple of allotment gardens, moved in with my mum and dad and started to build. It was at this time that we started to think about and talk about wanting a family. Until then it had been a totally out of the question alien possibility. Why does the light suddenly go on in the attic and our thoughts change?

I guess I was wondering what next? We'd had the exotic holidays, sat in the good job, bought expensive cars, passed the exams so there had to be more to life. Material things give a short, sharp burst but it is always temporary. In the whole scheme of things they are pretty meaningless really.

Shortly after moving to "Bryn Gwennol," – Swallow Hill for the uninitiated. We called it Swallow Hill because we had a swallows nest in the garage so we couldn't bring ourselves to put the doors on. The swallows nest fell down and I had a miscarriage. Little did I realise that in the not too distant future I would lie in The Swallow Suite at The University Hospital of Wales cradling baby Katie in my arms. Like butterflies swallows also play a part in my life and growth.

When things go wrong it brings you to your senses and you re-assess your priorities. The miscarriage happened the week after we came back from Israel. That was our thinking. Quick, let's have a holiday BC because we will not be able to go quite so far or quite so often with a baby. What a joke! We didn't get on a plane again for another decade. We always said that we preferred to go away in the caravan. Actually, it is peaceful and practical with children. Also we could only afford to go away in the caravan when I eventually became a full time Mum.

I was still waiting for the results of the pregnancy

test from the GP when I started to bleed. Was I pregnant? Why hadn't I done my own test? At least I would have known. When the bleeding became really heavy I pleaded with the Doctor to let me go to hospital. He said that there was no need and that I should collect anything of a reasonable size to show him. I am not good at multi- tasking and still don't see how you can deal with labour pains (if they were labour pains) and collect a gift for the Doctor. It's a relief that he doesn't want it gift wrapped! Eventually the Doctor agreed to make a house call and he phoned for an ambulance. On a Saturday night there was no ambulance available and, luckily, I still have never had a ride in an ambulance. Ivor took me to the Hospital in Merthyr Tydfil. His car was his pride and joy and I found myself silently praying firstly not to lose the baby. If I was to lose the baby it certainly couldn't happen in his precious car. I hadn't collected any goodies and I didn't have a "pressie" for the nurse so they promised to do a pregnancy test the next morning. I was given pethadine. The next morning there was no test. There was no urine, only blood. As there was nothing to test I needed a dilation and curettage (D+C). This is a surgical procedure to remove part of the lining and the contents of the uterus.

FIRST B.C.

THEN D+C.

I insisted Ivor went sailing while I was in theatre. I always worry about others and put their needs first. He could race his boat and still make visiting.

When I awoke Ivor was perched next to my bed. It would have been fine if there was a little crib the other side of the bed. There was nothing only an empty chair on one side and Ivor watching me. I found myself wondering how he must be feeling. I feel helpless so he must be having an even bigger dose of helplessness. It must be harder to watch someone going through a situation rather than experiencing it first- hand. I guess I should have asked him how he was feeling but I was afraid to hear what he might say. I was glad that Ivor had come empty handed as a box of chocolates or a bunch of flowers would have felt so empty. What if we can't have children? How soon can I go home and try for another baby? Why me? Why us? Why should we bother again? At least it would be fun practicing.

On Sunday night after my trip to theatre it was like re-living the whole experience again. In the middle of the night a young girl was admitted to the ward. She had a gift for the nurse that proved that she was no longer pregnant. I cried more that night in the darkness and silence of the ward than I had the night before. When I lived through the experience I felt frightened. Not only fear of the unknown and my ability to deal with the pain, but I had never been in hospital as a patient before. Now I was starting to cry for the little person we would never meet. A nurse caught me crying and scolded me as if she was dealing with a disobedient child. Like the words of the song I should have told her "It's my party (baby) and I'll cry if I want to, cry if I want to etc." I guess I was adding to her workload. I realise now that if I needed to cry then a box of tissues was permission enough. I should have worked through my feelings instead of going back to work less than a week later! Then, and now, I still have a lot to learn about the rule of this game they call life.

An Angel is Sent

Do you realise that you may not have met your best friends in life yet? When you meet certain people you may feel as if you have known each other for years. We may not feel worthy enough to have good friends and we may close our minds to the possibility of becoming friends with people out of our reach.

Career minded Anita would never have dreamed of sitting talking through very personal matters with Connie, the Counsellor at work. It may have a negative effect on my promotion prospects! After having the miscarriage I still didn't feel the need to talk, as colleagues suggested. In fact I was fine provided babies, hospital and anything maternal was not mentioned. I wasn't fine at all – "oh yes I was!" It sounds like a pantomime doesn't it? Life was a bit like that and it took one of the girls in the office to live through the same experience for me to fall apart, big time. When I fall apart I do it in style. I had taken over responsibility for staffing, training and managing the pay section that was to be opened in our Cardiff office. We all had to undergo training in London where the existing pay section lived. One day, in a training session we were going through very basic paperwork and form filling and it was just as if my brain ceased to function. It was frightening because I didn't connect my feelings to the grief I had denied. After all the miscarriage was history as it had happened several months before and it had not affected me in any way, shape or form. I got on the first available train and travelled home. The next morning I visited the GP and was prescribed anti- depressants. It all happened very quickly but the grieving process was slow and lasted many months. I felt sadness like never before. I didn't want to get up in the morning and I wanted to hide myself away in my bed as early as I could get away with.

Sometimes we are too close for comfort to a situation. We cannot see the wood for the trees and it takes a fresh pair of eyes to see what is happening. It was in these circumstances that the Counsellor became my friend. It was as if she knew what was going on in my mind. She also seemed to say all the right things and, most of the time this meant saying absolutely nothing at all. I felt MAD and my new friend really did "Make a Difference." She certainly helped me to get things back into perspective and stop blaming myself as I had done nothing wrong. When things settled down I realise that I would like to help others in the same way that I had been helped. My situation led me to deliver motivational training to the unemployed and help them back into work. I also attended the be-friender training with FSID. It made me realise that you have to understand your own feelings before you can even think of helping others .Who knows, maybe one day I will have the opportunity to work as a life coach, or in another capacity.

Some people just don't know what to say or do. Some crossed the road to avoid the embarrassment. There should be a few rules to help the grieving process. Instead of crossing the road, just STOP, LOOK, LISTEN and THINK. A nod and a smile would be fine as empathy is the key to the grieving door.

At that time the only thing that the Counsellor and I

had in common was my pain and suffering. I needed her support and her role was to get employees firing on all fours once more. Things changed a couple of years down the line. I was on maternity leave with Cooper and Connie had a new baby daughter. While on maternity leave and with the babies as a link our friendship grew so much so that she helped my whole family live through losing Katie and she came with me on every hospital visit when I was pregnant with Polly. We arranged my hospital visits only when Connie was free. You see I needed an interpreter. At the hospital my brain would suddenly empty of its own accord in much the same way I experienced when working in London after my miscarriage. I was back at "The Hospital," the one where I had all my check -ups when I was pregnant with Katie. The same staff, the same consultant, and still pregnant. I felt like an elephant – I think their pregnancies last a life time. They say elephants don't forget. I was the size of an elephant and I certainly hadn't forgotten the fact that Katie was born in the very same hospital.

I found the "hospital weighting room" an absolute nightmare. The conversations people had seemed so pointless. "I want a boy"..."I don't want a big baby." It was the same routine every time. Wait and weigh and wait some more. I tried not to listen to the chatter but the reality of the pregnancy weighed heavily on me. I shoulder the burden with as much courage and dignity as I can muster.

I was in danger of shouting "Shut up. I want a baby that breathes. I want to take a real, living baby that screams out of this place." Small talk, typical of a waiting room I know but I found listening to it a real challenge and very upsetting. My answer was to sit and cry. I know this was an extreme way of beating the queue but staff would wheel me away into privacy.

They were being kind to everyone as they wouldn't have wanted the "MAD" woman to upset others. I couldn't cope with waiting. The weight of the waiting room was just too heavy. The stress of waiting for Polly's arrival was about as much as I could bear. Please let her breathe, scream and live with us.

Ivor could have come to the hospital but, as usual, I thought of him and spared him the upsetting reminder. He attended the scan and put in an appearance at the birth, and I was fine with this. The scan drained all my energy and more. It is supposed to be a wonderful experience. Seeing the heartbeat reminded me that Katie's heart stopped beating. Everything had been fine at the scan stage with Katie. At 40 weeks everything was fine, so how can I relax this time. The radiographer asked "Would you like to know the sex of the baby, it may help?" I wanted to know and Ivor didn't. In my usual thoughtful way I told Ivor to go wait outside if he didn't want to hear because I needed to know. To get through, I needed to have any help that was available. From the radiographer's words I knew I was carrying a baby girl. I just wanted her to live, oh so very much. Polly Kate can never replace Katie. They are different children, but I think that a little girl must have helped dull the pain slightly. I wonder if we had been given the gift of another son whether there would have been another pregnancy in the Price- family. The scan should be emotional and exciting – seeing a new life. Ban the word "should" from the dictionary. It should be banned! It is not good to do anything because "you think you should." It is better to do what is right and what you want to do.

Many hospital visits and many months later Connie and I discussed Polly Kate's arrival. Yes she has a name and one baby-grow. That was the sum total of my preparation as I was too terrified to tempt fate. The consultant said we could try for "a normal delivery." I point blank refused. She has to scream and she has to be born on 31st August to enable me to go to the cemetery for Katie's first birthday on 13th September 1994. Polly was due on 14th September – how unreal is that? Surely, God was having a laugh and testing me to my limits.

I am stroppy and can be a feisty creature. I had a planned caesarean on 31st August 1994. Instead of waiting for a porter Polly and I walked to theatre as a couple, with Ivor close behind. I had my epidural while he was gowned and booted in his blue and white kit. Gwen, the midwife who confirmed that there was no heartbeat, delivered Katie and attended her funeral joined us in theatre. I really appreciated the fact she was up the talking end with me. I have had many years to think about Gwen's needs and the part her presence paid to heal her own grief. As Polly was lifted out the surgeon said "The cord is around her neck. What? If I had agreed to a "normal delivery I have no idea what the outcome may have been. Would Polly be living the life she lives today? Would she be riding race horses, winning races and keeping me on my toes? In any event I thank God I insisted on a planned caesarean. As soon as I saw Polly I didn't want to hold her. Seeing her was enough. The stresses and strains of the last two pregnancies could start to melt away. I wanted to turn over and sleep and sleep and sleep. Years later Polly is looking through her photograph album. Leather bound with her name in gold leaf on the front cover. She compares the first page of Cooper's album with page one of hers. She observes "When Cooper was born daddy didn't wear boy's nurse's clothes. He waited in the waiting room. He was dressed up when I was born so he must have been there with you, mum." After many hours of labour I had an emergency caesarean

61

with Cooper so it was entirely different. I was tired before having a general anaesthetic and I certainly wasn't thinking about the umbilical cord. Cooper arrived safely and I know nothing about the position of the umbilical cord. Ignorance certainly is bliss.

Connie was among the first of Polly's visitors. Thank you Connie! I will always be eternally grateful for Connie's friendship and support. God could have chosen someone else but I am so glad he chose you. I was in Connie's shadow and you can't live your life in someone else's shadow. As someone draws closer their shadow engulfs you and acts like a comfort blanket. If you stay in the shadows and grieve too long you may feel cold and lose the warmth and joy of living life to the full. Sunshine and shadows come and go in your life, just like friends, of that you can be certain. Don't stay too long grieving in the shadows. Certainly grieve, otherwise you will fall apart and miss the sunshine anyway. New friends will drop into your life. Embrace them, but never forget the good bits from old friendships. Try to look back on the past with as much pleasure as you can look forward to the future. Easy, when everything is plain sailing.

As Jonathan Swift said "Life is a comedy for him who thinks and a tragedy for him who feels." As you see people, they are. As you see the world, it is. As you see yourself you are. If you want to see the world differently or want to be treated differently, then change your glasses. Change the way you look at the world. My friendship with Connie changed when Connie went back to work. Other than Christmas cards, we don't really keep in touch. It is not so much as the end of a friendship but the end of an act or chapter in this thing called life. It is important to move on to the next chapter with your memories in place. Don't spend too long looking at the door that closed, otherwise you may fail to see the new door opening. You sometimes have to turn the page. You may even have to close the book for the last time and pass the book on to someone else.

Thank You
In this busy world in which we live
Sometimes filled with greed.
Most folk seem to rush on by
When someone has a need.
Unlike the Good Samaritan
Who stopped along the way?
We're all in such a hurry
To live each passing day.
Yet in this world of busy folks,
God sent a special one:
I'd like to take the chance to say
Thanks for all you've done.

(Author Unknown).

Connie was certainly my "Good Samaritan." How strange that when Polly was born I insisted to going to the church at the University Hospital of Wales. I remember looking at the Chaplin in awe when he started the reading. It was the story of the Good Samaritan. While my eyes darted form Polly to Ivor and then to the Chaplin Connie was in my thoughts.

Connie made and decorated Polly's baptism cake. White icing with a tiny, pale pink crib sitting on the top. It's a crib not a moses basket. Surprise, surprise she is Polly's Godmother. Polly was baptised at Pentyrch church and we all walked across the road to the Kings Arms. It was a light- hearted, fun afternoon. At one point I ended up behind the bar, at the sink washing glasses. Many people said that while looking at Polly they were also thinking of Katie and what might have been. I remember smiling with pleasure as I would have hated for Katie to be forgotten. She may be out of sight but she is not out of mind. I watch Cooper and his mates playing hide and seek. He is wearing green cords, a white shirt and a tiny "dicky- bow." He looks like a little grown up. I hope he hasn't had to grow up to quickly. I think back to Cooper's baptism. It was a much more formal affair. I was working full time so we could afford the same photographer as we had at our wedding. I confess that it was my idea and it was a total waste of money. The fact that I wanted to do things in style reflected on how I was before children (BC). Katie's baptism, sandwiched between the other two, was an entirely different affair. I sat up in bed wearing a hospital gown. Ivor, perched on the hospital bed, holds Katie his eyes are full, his heart is heavy and he is speechless. Together the Chaplin and I read the words in the order of service. Sometimes my tears blur the words and the Chaplin is on his own. I wipe my eyes, blow my nose and catch up. We don't race through the service but, in some ways, it is like a race between the Chaplin and me.

You shouldn't compare your children and I shouldn't compare the baptisms. Cooper's baptism certainly reflected life before children and Polly's reflected life today. Nothing will ever compare with Katie's. It is beyond compare. What she has done for the whole family is beyond compare and, as I type, I listen to "The Rose" playing in the background.

Tea and Sympathy

Friends crawled out of the woodwork armed with bunches of flowers and grapes. I guess people agonised over the appropriate gift to bring when a baby dies. You cannot empathise, sympathise or prophesise unless you have a cup in your hand. The Welsh translation reads "cwpaned o de." The more tea I drank the more milk I produced. "Big babilons," as Ali G would say, are painful when there is no baby suckling. Diane, the midwife whom cared for me when I was pregnant with Cooper, Katie and Polly had a brilliant idea. She suggested I have a cup of tea with the visitors who came to sympathise, but I should only drink half. Wow, I would never have thought of that. I know half souls don't go to heaven but, it halved my discomfort. I often wondered why they didn't give you something to dry up the milk. I guess my body didn't know that my baby had died. If nature is so clever why couldn't she work this out? They can put a man on the moon, so why should I have to wear wet, milk- stained, baggy tee-shirt? It was a constant reminder of the baby I wasn't allowed to feed. I felt as if my body had failed Katie. It is not as if I wasn't prepared to breast feed. It is the best start in life you can give your baby, if it is possible for you. You also have an excuse to put your feet up and have a cup of tea. There was nothing I would have loved more than to have cuddled and fed baby Katie. I wasn't allowed the privilege. Maybe God thought that He could do a better job.

Enter centre stage Dr. Lewis. She didn't come armed with lectures but she oozed sympathy and genuine understanding. Many years ago she had lost a baby so she knew exactly how I felt. It is so true that you cannot describe a place you haven't been. Holiday snaps are great but nothing compared to going on holiday. We had a customary "cwpaned," hugged and shed genuine tears of sheer understanding. She is a brilliant Doctor. She always seems to know exactly what I need. I really wish she had been looking after me when I had the miscarriage. The Doctor who looked after me was from a different practice because we had moved house. He may as well have come from a different planet. Maybe he was from Mars and Dr. Lewis is certainly a Venus resident. He didn't understand how terrified I was and he did no more than he had to. My philosophy in life is that we should go the extra mile whenever there is an opportunity.

We have only a small number of photographs of Katie to remember her short stay with us. Each of the children have a white leather photograph album with their name and date of birth embossed in gold on the front cover. Katie has the same white album as Cooper and Polly and you may think that I am "MAD" but it really has made a difference to me. I remember the day the album arrived in the post. I was cleaning to get rid of the day, as you do when your world has fallen apart. The cleaner sat alone in the centre of the room while I arranged and re-arranged the contents of Katie's album. There is not much at all:

A Polaroid photograph taken soon after she was born.
A professional photograph given as has a gift from the

hospital.
A lock of hair.
Hand and footprints.
A bonnet made for her arrival.
(No ties as there was no time for my
Mum to sew them on.)
Sympathy cards and letters.
Magazine and newspaper cuttings to remind me that I
am not alone.

As I hold her tiny bonnet in my hands I picture my mum sitting by the fire knitting. The wool is so soft and pure white. When I came home from hospital I realised that I didn't have the bonnet. I phoned the hospital and arranged to call in to collect it. Usually I just get on with things but I couldn't, I just couldn't face it. In my mind I could picture the nurses' station on the maternity ward. I didn't want to re-visit the place as the memories were much too raw. I delayed. I stayed close to my own mum and to my son, Cooper. He was my greatest comfort at the time. It took me many weeks to visit the maternity ward. When I did I relived the whole experience. I remember telephoning the hospital to say that I wasn't aware of the baby moving. The builder was working and there was the noise of drilling in the background. The lady I spoke to said that she could hear the panic in my voice. She calmly said to come into the hospital for them just to check that everything was fine. I drove into Cardiff not realising that Cooper's car seat was in the back of the car. When I arrived I was shown into a room and they checked for the heartbeat on the monitor. Then they placed an old fashioned trumpet on my abdomen and swiftly turned the monitor away from me. One nurse, standing at the bottom of the bed said "baby has gone." I can picture her now standing at the foot of the bed with her hands in her pockets and wearing a thick knitted cardigan. She was looking at the monitor when she spoke so had no eye contact with me. It sounded so cruel and so matter of fact, but I guess it was straight to the point and there wouldn't be a kind way of breaking the news. What should she have said? What could she have said? Maybe she should have turned on her heels, left quietly and allowed the nurse closest to me to look at me, talk to me and give me her undivided attention. She couldn't give me hope but I deserved attention.

Which room was I shown into to telephone Ivor to get him to the hospital? I was economical with the truth when I phoned because he had to drive to the hospital safely. He had to wait for my parents to arrive. My mum stayed at the building site to look after Cooper and my dad drove Ivor to the hospital so that Ivor could drive my car home. All of this took time and all the while I was sitting in the office talking to Gwen, the midwife who would play a part in my life over the next twelve months. Gwen said that I was a born actress and Ivor wouldn't have realised the size of the problem we were facing. At the time I was thinking of Ivor and the situation he would have to deal with. Did we always used to think of each other, work things through and change together? No, I always thought of Ivor and put his needs first. We grieved in our own ways and we have certainly changed. I guess the key is to make sure you change in the same direction if your relationship is to remain solid.

Your baby is broken.
Your baby cannot be repaired.
Prepare yourself to be induced.
The sign above the bed said "Nil by Mouth."
Ivor was given sandwiches.
Ivor slept on a bean bag.

Ivor stayed the whole time.
God Bless you Ivor
Thank you for staying.
Katie arrives
She was stillborn
SHE WAS STILL BORN
Her album says so
The gold lettering reads
"Katie Price 13th September 1993."

Katie's birth wasn't all doom and gloom. We knew that there was no heartbeat. My worst fears had been confirmed when I was conscious that she wasn't moving. When Ivor arrived at the hospital he was shown into the office and he stood and just looked at me. We hugged while I cried until I was all cried out and then I cried some more. I was allowed to go home and gather a few things for what lay ahead. Walking down the hospital steps I remember breathing deeply. I remember the fresh cool air on my face and I just wished that I didn't exist. The thought of the ordeal ahead was just too much. My Community midwife met me at my parent's house and her words of wisdom certainly helped prepare me mentally. She gave me courage and strength as she explained that we would be encouraged to agree to a post- mortem even before baby put in an appearance. Sitting in the living room with my mum and the midwife I wanted to sit there forever without moving or speaking. I didn't want to go back to the hospital and yet I knew I had no choice. Like a criminal running from the scene of the crime I wondered if they would send out a search party. Ivor encourages me to stop playing statues and to get into the car. The journey takes a lifetime and every light is red but I don't want to get there and I can't wait to get there all at once. We were shown to our room, just like checking into a hotel. Without delay the midwives got on with their job and I was induced. Just a little gel on the cervix and then they set up an epidural. Am I really sitting up on a bed cuddling a pillow as I arch my back as the anaesthetist hits the spot? I was hot and I guess that they didn't have to keep the delivery room warm for Katie's appearance. I can picture Ivor now, perched up the talking end with his coat on and his collar up around his neck with the gentle breeze from the fan ruffling his hair. He had hair then! The nurses wore thick jackets and the "winter woollies" they'd knitted on quieter nights. In those days Ivor was cool. He sat there rubbing his hands together to try to warm them and says "I guess I now know how Biggles felt!" I didn't know how he felt I just know that I was burning up, boiling hot and not allowed to eat or drink. I vaguely remember a burning sensation which the midwife explained indicated the time had come to start pushing. She called it the "ring of fire" created by the baby's head bearing down. I think baptism by fire would be more accurate and appropriate. I am burning up and yet I am still picturing the birth plan I so lovingly put together. As Cooper was born by an emergency caesarean after a long and difficult labour I really wanted it to be as natural as possible this time. I wouldn't go as far as to say no pain relief but I had already had the gel and the epidural and now nature brings out a ring of fire. Any minute now I am going to ask for a caesarean. Instead they are shouting and counting. Push 1, 2, 3, 4, and 5. "Well done, good girl, we will soon see baby's head."If this is a quiz I have failed dismally! No points awarded for a baby who cannot cry. I can't say there were no complications as the whole situation was complicated into a world of disbelief. If I cry will it make a difference? My eyes are so dry that they are painful. I'm tired and I don't want to play this game anymore. There is no prize at the end of the game, at least not one that I would be allowed to take home.

The room is cold and Katie is small. I still have to be cut before Katie arrives without a cry. On the next push they cut and I am not even aware of what is happening. That is so unfair. Not that I don't know what is happening but that I have to be cut. She is placed straight on to my tummy. I look at her stillness and I take in every detail. Ten fingers and ten toes and she is, just so perfect. I lift her up onto my chest so I can take a closer look. She is lying there but not crying and, in silence they stitch me.

They want to take her away and I want to keep her. It is not as if they are planning to take her to the special baby care unit. It has all the equipment that you can imagine but no amount of innovation or dreaming will let them resuscitate our brand new baby. She is a brand of her very own and I want to watch her grow up and become her own person. The saying "a stitch in time saves nine," drops into my mind. Why, couldn't something have happened to alert me to the problem? The stitches the midwife so deftly sewing now, are for me but why couldn't I have been given the tiniest clue, early enough to save my girl? Why? I am oblivious to what is happening to my body. I feel numb so I cannot feel a thing. Labour has been spread over two days and the epidural has taken the edge off the physical pain. I am tired but I cannot sleep. I am running through the events of the day over and over again. If anything I feel hyper- active and I continue to talk to the midwife. I ask her numerous questions and I convince her that baby Katie must stay at my side in her Moses basket. It is very colourful, suitable for a baby boy or girl. I wish it was white but, more to the point, I wish Katie was alive. I guess this is the Moses basket they keep in the cupboard for these occasions. Sleep eludes me and I am wheeled, in my bed to "The Swallow Suite and Ivor walks alongside. In the safety of the four walls I cuddle Katie and the nurse waits to place her in her Moses basket. She waits and she waits and we chat and we chat some more.

I can't sleep
I keep looking at the Moses basket
This isn't fair.
Ivor sleeps peacefully.
Ivor sleeps like a baby.
Sleep eludes me.
I refuse a sleeping tablet.
I prefer to chat to the nurse
I chat about nothing and everything.
Sleep will knock on my door.
I will talk myself to sleep.
The nurse may fall asleep first.
How can Ivor sleep?
I am afraid to sleep because I snore loudly.
My snoring cannot wake Katie
I want to go to sleep and not wake up
This is unreal.
Goodnight brand new baby girl.
My special little lady.
Goodnight.

Plain Sailing

"Before children" (BC) you tend to take a good night's sleep for granted. With this and everything else Ivor and I were totally self- centred. We booked holidays last minute and flew to warmer climes whenever an opportunity presented itself. We both worked hard building our home together and laying the foundation of our careers. I thought I had arrived when the Civil Service not only gave me day release to study, paid my course fees but also threw my expenses into the bargain. The number of hours I spent studying was irrelevant because I was building my CV – BC.

Looking back studying was like a drug to me. Having dropped out of college because I was homesick and hated the geography degree I was studying – I had to prove to myself that I wasn't thick. "A Level" geography had been a doddle – hard work, but o.k. if you were prepared to swot yourself silly. The degree course was a different ball game. You needed to be able to read a map, have a sense of direction and a love of the great out-doors was essential. I can see me now wading in a river, measuring its velocity in a dark, dark wood in the early hours. Not for the faint hearted and not for anyone who cannot navigate herself out of a paper bag. Fighting back tears and mascara running down my face was just not a pretty sight or a long term option.

It was soon after dropping out of college that I met

Ivor. Although, at the time, I was going out with his friend I was drawn to him. We saw each other once a week and soon became inseparable. Within the year we were married. For the honeymoon we went on a mini cruise to Denmark. The sea was rough, the bunk beds caused a bit of a stir but it was also a sign of the many hours I would spend at sea with Ivor!

We sailed together. Would you believe I even learnt to swim to go sailing with Ivor? I have never gone so far as to get my face wet. I am a cleanser girl and even shut my eyes in the shower. I swim like a swan and dread the day that Polly asks me to blow bubbles in the water. Both Cooper and Polly are good swimmers. Cooper surfs and Polly has been diving. In this respect, I have to admit that they follow their father.

Ivor had a long succession of two- man and finally a single handed boat. It looks especially weird upside down on a roof rack. A bit like a baby Concorde that has just belly dived out of the sky to park nicely on the roof of our vehicle. Nicely balanced on the roof rack and the same applies on the water if she is to fly and win the race. I think that we can apply the same principle to ourselves. I found it heavy weather when Cooper was born because I suffered with post- natal depression. I guess that it was worse because I didn't realise that I was ill. When you are depressed it is not that you don't feel good or bad. You just don't feel anything other than numb. Although I love Cooper to bits and spent hours just looking at him and drinking in his every detail the weather was heavy and I was broken. I struggled to eat and food was just like chewing sawdust. A few hours of sleep terminated in the early hours. I would lie there with a sense of foreboding and would worry about what the day ahead had in store for me. In light winds you go nowhere and may even drift backwards. You have to weather the storm at sea and in your life. When you have travelled through a storm and look back, you have probably learned more than when things were plain sailing. Watch the highs, they may signal a low. Watch the boat's tiller. Check that the following wind is favourable. Remember this is exactly when there is danger of going off course. Smooth sailing, when all is well may make you complacent.

To go fast in life you need to be well balanced. You don't want "burn out" or "rust out." Balance in life means that things are in proportion and your life is just the right fit for you. A car drives better when the wheels are balanced. Balance makes our life larger. Imbalance makes our lives smaller. Ivor now sails a cruiser. It has an engine and a propeller and together they are both essential. Taken by itself the engine would sink and the propeller would also sink. Together they achieve more than they would individually. Ivor and I are like this. Together we have great synergy and, through rough seas and when the sea is calm we work well as a team. I really think that after losing Katie that nothing can come between us and we can deal with anything. Time alone will tell and I will either be proved right or wrong on this one.

Is your life balanced and on course? Do you feel that you are sinking, swimming or struggling to stay afloat in this difficult economic climate? Are you swimming with the tide or fighting against it? Maybe it is time to think about making some changes in our lives. Imagine yourself as a cookie jar. The jar is full of a freshly baked selection of cookies –chocolate, raisin, nut and oatmeal to name just a few. They are warm and yummy. You love these cookies because you have baked them yourself. You have made them and you wish to share them with others. As the cookies are eaten and enjoyed you simply make more. This is not tiring because it gives you great pleasure. Several weeks later your cookies have gained a reputation. They are still everything that they were before, but they are being eaten faster and faster. As fast as they are being eaten you have a job to replace them. People are taking advantage and taking a handful of cookies and passing them on to friends.

Six months later the jar is not always full, or when it is, it only has one or two flavours. You have resorted to getting up earlier to fit in extra baking. Now you realise that you don't bake with love, care and attention anymore. It is a chore. The biscuits don't taste as good. What has gone wrong? Is life out of balance? Are you near "burn out" or "rust out?"

When Cooper was born in 1991 life was a little out of balance to say the least. We had to make a few adjustments to our life. It appeared to me that Ivor's life went on much the same as usual. He left for work "looking like the bees knees," in his suit and carrying his brief case containing his sandwiches. I was still in my dressing gown at lunchtime wondering why I felt ill because I hadn't eaten. Why could I run a busy office but I couldn't get Cooper to fit in with my study schedule? Was I missing something? I was studying for my final exams to gain membership of the Chartered Institute of Personnel and Development (CIPD). I guess motherhood and studying are not a good mix and my life was just a little out of balance. I yet had to make the shift from the world of the busy office and the office politics to the world of breast feeding, sleepless nights and the special scent of a brand new baby. I often wonder how I would deal with all of this now, post Katie. I would probably tell them to stuff their office politics and parties to be free to savour my family and have fun with them.

Cooper took ages to make an appearance and the

birth had been traumatic. Baby was in a posterior position and labour failed to progress. I kept demanding pethadine and anything else I could persuade them to give me. I really believed the pethadine did nothing for me, even when Ivor relays the things I said to the Consultant. I raised myself up on the bed and said "Leave it another 30 minutes before making a decision – you should be laying here mate!" They decide to take another look inside and the curtain parts and enter centre stage the orange cleaning fluid to start the procedure. I sigh, I glower, I roll my eyes and I say "I must have the cleanest fanny in Merthyr Tydfil!" Anybody who knew me at the time would think this is totally out of character for Anita. Today it would not be out of character as I am feisty and I speak my mind. The cookie jar of my life has taught me to be true to myself. This linked with a couple of shots and super glued to the gas and air would give carte blanche approval to be stroppy.

My depression was aggravated by the fact that I was afraid to admit how I was feeling. How should you feel? I thought everything would be fine when I went back to work when Cooper was six months old. After all I loved work, the office politics and trips to London. I didn't want to go and I certainly didn't want to leave Cooper. My mother gave up her job in the school kitchen I know she only worked a couple of hours a day but it is an amazing thing to do. Although it gave me peace of mind and I had no worries about leaving Cooper I just didn't want to go to work. I felt physically sick driving to work each day. The work I once found so scintillating seemed so pointless, fruitless and just a pain in the neck. It didn't give me the satisfaction it used to. The cookie jar was empty and I didn't want it replenished. I didn't want to be anywhere. I just didn't want to be. I had closed down emotionally. I just wanted to enjoy life again and never gave up hope of a brighter tomorrow. If you had given me a million pounds I wouldn't have felt any better. I wouldn't have felt anything. That is what depression is like. Every problem felt overwhelming and there was never a solution in sight.

When I found out that I was pregnant with Katie the sparkle came back into my eyes. When Cooper's baby brother or sister arrives I would be a full time mum. I would have a toddler and a new baby to justify staying at home, spending my days playing with them both. Katie wasn't allowed to play but I walked away from my well paid job to grieve in peace. I didn't have to put on an act each day. I also had quality time with Cooper before Polly joined us on 31st August 1994 – less than a year after Katie's funeral. I wouldn't say that Polly's arrival made life plain sailing but it eased the pain further.

I knew that there would be no more babies and I also knew that Ivor was headed for the snip. I remember making an appointment with Dr Lewis to talk about this. She said Ivor would need to be involved! She also suggested that I was sterilised so that I would be in control of my own fertility. Why would I want to do that? Surely, I had been through enough. In the fullness of time I may realise that I should have listened to Dr Lewis' advice. Ivor had the snip. I smiled and seemed to drive over every pothole after his day surgery. I wish I had been sterilised. One thing is certain, you never know what then future has in store for you.

Ivor usually sailed on a Sunday as it was his day of rest after a week at work. I didn't have a day of rest. My first job was to deposit Cooper safely at Sunday school. He is excited because the full dress rehearsal day for the Nativity play has arrived. In his rucksack he has a tea towel for his head and a sheep to cuddle. You have guessed, he is a shepherd and I have never seen a group of little boys with such wonderful nurturing skills.

Polly and I head to the supermarket. Polly is able to sit up so she views the world from her supermarket trolley. Some of the trolleys have a shelf just above the floor - a "trolley cot" for babies to inhale dust from the floor. If I had Katie there is no way she would have slept and swept the floor at the same time, while I shopped. I swear, I stomp and I feel real anger. Why should these Mothers have their babies when they use them to sweep the floor while I wasn't allowed to keep Katie? Still raging within, I proceed to the check out. We proceed to the door and a security guard puts his hand on my shoulder and stops me in my tracks. We are taken into a small room and they show me the new born baby clothes on the shelf I begin to tell the store manager about SARA. I have a friend called Sara who I love dearly but I am not talking about her. I am talking about the model I use which relates to managing change in general and the grieving process in particular. The initial feeling of Shock is replaced by Anger, then Resentment and eventually Acceptance. I fall way short from accepting the situation I find myself in. Whilst my behavior in the supermarket has shocked me it doesn't compare with the shock I felt at the hospital when they turned the monitor away and told me there was no heartbeat. My heart was beating like a drum fit to burst. I felt hot, sick and nervous all at once as I see the baby clothes perched just above the floor. Why would I want the baby clothes when I don't have a new-born? A couple of months ago the clothes would have fitted Polly. Yesterday they would have fitted Polly, today they do not and I wonder who they will fit tomorrow.

The Security Guard and the Store Manager listen to

me going on. I insist that I need to pick Cooper up from Sunday school. I leave my shopping trolley and I am allowed to collect Cooper but I must return. All the time Ivor is oblivious to my adventure as he is racing his sailing dinghy. Where else would he be on a Sunday morning? On our return we are bundled into a police car. The Christmas before Cooper had asked for fifteen pairs of handcuffs so imagine his excitement having a ride in a police car. I don't remember whether the blue light and siren was on. I felt tired, numb and angry. I shouted at the store manager and told him what I thought of the trolley design.

At the police station a young police woman cuddled Polly and arranged for a drink of squash for each of them. Cooper visited the cells but wasn't keen to go in by himself! Cooper had done nothing wrong and he got to see the inside of a cell. I was the criminal and I only visited the interview room and had my finger prints taken. The police officer spent time talking to me and asking why I had behaved in this way. I explained about Katie and told him how unfair life was. If I had been allowed to keep Katie she would never have viewed the supermarket at floor level. The kind copper in his smart uniform suggested that I should arrange to talk to someone but that it would be best not to mention it today. He was trying to tell me that if I talk, think and act like a crazy person it would need to be mentioned in their report. Instead I need to get help and get sorted and get on with my life. You don't need to know the name of the supermarket I was banned from, but I took my ban seriously. More than eighteen years later and I have never been in-store again. Today, I look nothing like I did then. My hair is a different colour and style and I am no longer a thin stick insect.

A caution and another ride in a police car and we are at the supermarket car park to collect my car. We are now late for Sunday lunch at my Mum's and I wonder how I will explain away my lateness. Cooper bounds in and tells my mum about the ride in the police car. I giggle and say, "He has a vivid imagination!" My mum accepts this as she remembers the helping me in the quest to purchase the handcuffs. She giggles and I blush about my lie. It takes me ten years to tell Ivor and my mum about my criminal record. I feel so ashamed and it is so out of character for me. They seem to understand as I guess most people would. There was a reason for my behaviour and I needed help.

Several years late I find myself working with unemployed young adults. Some have alcohol or drug problems and have been in trouble with the police. I have a better understanding of their situation as I have been in a police car but not in a police cell. At least not yet! I really believe that every experience, whether positive or negative, can allow us to grow if we learn from the situation. Just thinking of those gorgeous men in uniform brings a smile to my face. Also as I walk past the supermarket, the one I am banned from, the design of the trolley has changed and there is no shelf scraping just above the ground. See, my mission was not in vain and I brought about a change. I'm sure, with a little thought, I could have taken a better and certainly a legal approach, rather than breaking the law and making us late for Sunday lunch! Another bigger thing I learned is that Ivor and my mum didn't judge me. They didn't shout at me or love me less. Maybe I am too judgemental. I judged the supermarket and the mothers who dared to use the shelf as newborn storage.

Many years later I pluck up the courage to tell Cooper and Polly. As I am sharing my story with the world, I thought I should. Cooper remembered it but Polly was just a baby herself. They both giggle and I remind them that they do not need to go shoplifting to learn right from wrong. You can learn from other peoples' mistakes without getting into trouble yourself. The supermarket made a change and I have not been in a police car since.

The Fishing Competition Crashed

Polly's birthday falls in the school holidays, just before the start of term so whilst we have a small party away on holidays, Polly's main party takes place with her school friends when we are back at home. As usual Ivor avoided the party and took the caravan to get a damp test organised at the caravan hospital. The workshop closed at seven so surprise, surprise, I expected Ivor to be with us by the time I had taken the children home. When I eventually got home there was a message on the answer-phone to say that he would be a little late and would ring back. I knew there was nothing to worry about as he would be putting the world to rights at the Caravan Hospital.

An hour or so later Ivor rang to say that he needed a lift home. "Fine, from where?" I asked. "From casualty," he replied. The nurse gave me instructions to find casualty. Ivor didn't know because he has been taken in on a stretcher with his head in "chocs." A fifty-two seater bus had crashed into the back of the caravan, written the caravan off and bent the Disco chassis. Thank God the caravan was there to take the brunt of the shock. I dread to think what the outcome might have been otherwise.

All the way to the hospital, with tears in my eyes, I prepared the children for how dad may look. We are on our way to the fateful hospital where Katie was born. He may have a collar on, be wearing bandages or have

83

something in plaster. Oh God, will he be able to walk to the car? I had better park as close as I can just in case he can't walk. My mind was working overtime and I was automatically thinking the worst, as we do. The saying "ignorance is bliss" is quite true. Our mind stays safely on its lead until the lead is removed allowing it to go on the rampage.

When you are having a good time it is true that time flies and when we are worried or frightened it is as if time stands still. The journey seemed to last a life time and, to make things even worse; every traffic light was on red. Again we can learn a lot from our children because neither Cooper nor Polly wasted energy worrying about their dad; after all, he must be fine as we were collecting him and taking him home. Cooper talked about the rugby game he had played and Polly sang about her birthday party.

Not only could Ivor walk but, miraculously he had no bandages, collar or plaster. He was quite stiff and had a whiplash injury which, he had been told, would get worse over the next 48 hours. As Ivor said, "You don't have a bus up your backside and get away scot free." The next morning we dropped Cooper and Polly in school and went to the Caravan Hospital. We emptied the caravan in the rain and you wouldn't believe the amount of essential junk we had in there. We have baggage to carry in our lives so it follows that the same applies to our home and even the caravan. Once I accepted that Ivor was okay and was breathing anyway I started going on about the "dirty weekend" we had planned for just a couple of days time. We were meant to be going to a plush campsite with a sauna, jacuzzi and steam room. When you have young children it is important to have quality time together. We had to delay our weekend for a couple of weeks but the whole episode got me thinking. It made me realise just how important the special people in your life are. If they can be put back together again and be bandaged that it wonderful but no amount of bandage could have helped Katie. It would have been too little too late. All the dirty weekends in the universe could be postponed, cancelled or deleted if Katie could be here with me. The caravan trauma and the time at the Caravan Hospital made me realise that the people in my life are important. Material things will never have a hold over me but, I have to admit that handbags would have to be excluded from this category.

The family who play together stay together and I hope this is the case for us. Teamwork is the key. Cooper uses Polly's hair bobbles to hold the line in place on his fishing reel. When Ivor has running repairs to do on his boat he uses my hairdryer to dry the gel coat. When my hairdryer isn't in the bedroom I just fetch it from the garage. Team can be described as "Together Each Achieves More." I would describe team as fishing, hairdryer, garage and hair bobbles! If Katie was here with us I wonder which extra item would be included. In guess I would include glue because, at times of trauma and life is all trouble and strife Katie's memory makes us stop, take a rain check and she glues the team together. Thank you once again Katie Price.

It was the day of Cooper's third fishing competition. After the accident Ivor's body was slowly seizing and sitting for the duration of a fishing competition was out of the question. He had been told not to drive, so it made sense for me to take Cooper fishing. One team member is substituted for another. I didn't have much to do as Cooper always sorts out his own gear. We've tried to teach both Cooper and Polly to take responsibility for their things. At least this avoids me getting it in the neck when things go wrong. We have to be responsible for what we do and to be able to live with the outcome and accept the consequences of our actions. If he forgets to take some of his fishing gear it is down to him. Have you ever seen the word "responsibility" split into two "response" and "ability?" You have the ability to choose how you respond in any given situation. If you too forget the fishing gear, (or something important to you) - it is up to you whether you respond or react. Often we over react and lose the plot. I am certainly guilty of this and I am sure this is a life- long lesson for me.

Once the fishing gear is packed it's off to the tackle shop. He makes his own shopping list, but we pay! I packed my own bag; a book to read, cross stitch to sew, chocolate to keep our seratonin levels up and various other goodies to eat. Also my deck chair, a warm coat and hat, my wellies, an umbrella and my sun cream! Years ago I was in the Brownies; you have to be prepared. I take more gear than Cooper and I don't take part in the fishing competitions.

I guess there is an art in travelling light. Can you pack one suitcase for a two week holiday? If you were back packing around the globe, could you fit all you need into a carrier bag? I believe we carry too much baggage in life. We need to let go of past hurts, put down our baggage and learn to forgive. It is the only way you can move on in life. Remember, if you carry baggage that is too heavy you get tired!

Have you ever heard the story of the old man and young boy who lived in ancient times? The old man was named Sartebus and the young boy was named Kim. The old man was looking for a place to sleep and Kim was looking for reason. "Why" he wondered "do we travel throughout our lives in search of something we cannot find? Why must things be so difficult? Do we make things difficult? These are big thoughts for a young boy to carry. Throughout their journey together the old man carried a big basket. Kim, being a thoughtful boy, offered to carry Sartebus' basket. However tired he was he would never accept help. Why are some of us so independent? He always insisted "This is something that I must carry for myself. One day you will walk your own road and carry a basket as weighted as mine." Over many days and many roads they walked together until Sartebus could walk no more. At last he shared with Kim what was in his basket. "In this basket," Sartebus said, "are all the things I believed about myself which were not true. They are the stones that weighed down my journey. On my back I have carried the weight of every pebble of doubt, every grain of sand of uncertainty, and every milestone of misdirection I have collected along my way." With that the old man closed his eyes and quietly went to sleep for the last time. Before Kim went to sleep that night he untied the cord that bound the basket to the old man and set him free. When he looked inside the basket that had weighed Sartebus down for so long he saw that it was empty!

There has to be a moral to this story. Just don't let the trials of life weigh you down and hold you back. Instead, change the way you look at them. Put down the baggage you carry. Let the past rest where it should; leave it behind you and move on. The key is to let go of the past but not to forget what you can learn from it. The way I remember this is to picture myself holding a coin tightly in my hand. If I open my hand and let the coin drop to the floor I have lost everything. If, instead, I open my hand with my palm turned upwards, I let go of the coin because I am no longer holding it tightly but I still have the coin to spend. I can learn from the experiences I've had without letting them grip me so tightly that they hold me back.

I walked to the lake laden like a pack horse, just showing that I've still got a lot to let go of in life and sometimes my baggage is just too much to carry. I guess this is true for the majority of us. Cooper never offers to carry my gear because, as you know, we are all responsible for the garbage we carry in life. The competition started at 9.00a.m. By 9.30 only one other lad had arrived and Cooper was already well into his fishing. We didn't see any organisers, there was no competition but Cooper just got on with the job in hand. We can learn so much from our children. He said nothing negative and took the opportunity to get in some extra practice. He studied the lake, decided where there seemed to be the most action and got on with it. Big people would have fretted about the fact that no one else was there and wasted the great opportunity while we giggled and put the world to rights. What a waste of energy.

I saw this as a golden opportunity to sit and chat to Cooper. No interruptions, like the telephone, television or door bell and such a beautiful setting - green trees, green murky water, green fishermen sitting on a green fishing box. They look as if they are in fancy dress. The setting would make you green with envy. I tried to guess how Cooper would answer if asked "what do you like about fishing?" If I'd taken the opportunity to ask him I might have found out. For me the calm, peaceful setting gave me the opportunity to chat to Cooper and think about the traumas of the last days so I could put them to rest. What can I learn from today? What is Cooper teaching me about his approach to life?

It was fun watching the father and son team who had

turned up for the competition. The dad was a keen fisherman himself and he wouldn't let the lad unpack the fishing gear. In a competition they always draw lots for the peg you sit at. It is the only fair way to ensure that no one has an unfair advantage. Ignorance is bliss and I am glad that I am often oblivious. They stood and watched, and watched us until they phoned home to say what was happening. They stayed for an hour or so, talking work on the mobile until eventually the light went on in the attic and Dad decided to set up a rod and fish as well. Every minute that was lost fretting about the unfairness of the situation was lost forever. They were putting more garbage in their fishing boxes by the minute? How long and how far will they carry the baggage of the day with them? The lost minutes will never be repeated again or stored until the sun shines. At about lunch time I was thinking about asking Cooper if he wanted a sandwich when he said "I don't think the competition is going to be on, do you? Anyway, let's stay until the maggots run out. I guess there is a moral in this story as well! You have to deal with what life throws at you and just get on with it. This is exactly what Cooper did. After all, it was only a fishing competition that hadn't taken place. This is a bit different from the cancellation of his baby sister's arrival. A delay is one thing but a cancellation is much more to deal with. Cooper dealt with the cancelled "comp" and as a team the whole family is still dealing with Katie's cancellation and Polly's arrival less than a year later. The caravan accident is minor in the whole scheme of things. Sometimes life poses one hell of a big scheme to get our heads around. Speaking from experience, with support, you can deal with anything life throws at you.

Follow the Children

"Rub a dub dub
Katie's shrub in a tub
And where do you think it went?"

The day of Katie's first birthday we celebrated in style. It was 13th September 1994 and Polly was just thirteen days old. The figure one and three certainly figure in our lives. Katie was born on the 13th and Polly was born on 31st. Swap the numbers around and move one year forward and you have a winner. I will never see the number 13 as unlucky. I know Katie died on the 13th but she was also born on 13th and she made a difference. When something really significant happens in my life, more often than not, the date is the 13th. Many years ago I would have thought this to be no more than a pile of nonsense. "Katie, you have changed me and my outlook." I don't care if people think I am barking mad and one crazy lady, but Katie made such a difference to the way I operate. It is no surprise that I have dawdled over this book. At times typing hasn't come easy and I have had to dig deep within. It is no surprise that I have waited until 2013 to share my thoughts and feelings with the world.

To celebrate we went to lunch and afterwards to the garden centre to buy a tiny shrub. We took pains to find one that flowers in September. A tiny, pale pink flower; not a rose, I may add. When we moved to live by the sea in Saundershoe we dug up Katie's shrub, planted it in a tub and took it on a road trip down West. Katie's ashes are still buried at Glyntaff Cemetery near Pontypridd. I know Katie's soul is not buried underground but, I am pleased that she is not alone. When my Dad died, we decided to bury his ashes with Katie. He is the new kid on the block cradling his grand -daughter in his arms. I have to smile as a picture of the tiny piece of stone they share pops into my mind. Yes, it has both sets of names and dates but there also is a teddy bear to keep Katie company. She now has my Dad and they both have a teddy bear. My Dad had been ill for a long time and no more could be done. A couple of months after he died I went for a psychic reading. I really wanted confirmation that he had settled in his new home. I know that in the world of spirit our illness is no more and we are restored to the best of health. The clairvoyant confirmed this. I also knew that she was talking about my dad because she said he was pleased that none was late for his funeral. To say that he was a stickler for time is an understatement. She continued to tell me that he had two small children with him. I could understand that Katie could be perched on his knee but, but, but! She explains that there is an older boy and a younger little girl. My eyes fill with tears and I realise that she is talking about the baby I miscarried all that time ago. I always felt that it was a boy and we lovingly referred to him as Tom because he was the size of a thumb nail. My mouth is open, my eyes are leaking and I am at a loss for words. One thing is certain I feel a huge weight lifted off my shoulders knowing that Tom and Katie are with my dad in the world of spirit. My psychic friend looks at me and says "You do know that she didn't want to leave you, don't you?" I nod and from somewhere deep down I know that Katie didn't have a choice and that Katie had to leave. She had done her special job and she had changed many people as part of the process.

When my dad died my mum moved to Saundershoe so she is close to her family and not alone either. We bought a bungalow in Saundershoe. We needed a big tin opener to raise the roof and make it into a house. Most people would have bought a house but we are not most people. Why take the easy option? Will I ever learn to take the easy option?

I believe that you don't have to give your children fancy presents that cost a fortune. I have a fridge magnet that says that you need to give children "roots to grow and wings to fly." Not much then? Actually something huge. Anything we give from the heart is always huge. It is important to let go. After losing Katie we could have been over- protective with Cooper and Polly. We could have wrapped them in cotton wool, but you have to have faith that everything will work out. You may not get the outcome you want but you have to let go. Polly rides races and I feel terrified as I watch her fly past. She has to follow her heart and do what she wants. She does and I love her for it. The poem entitled "Let Go and Let God" sums it up nicely:

> "As children bring their broken toys
> With tears for us to mend
> I brought my broken dreams to God
> Because He was my friend
> But instead of leaving Him
> In peace to work alone
> I hung around and tried to help
> With ways that were my own.
> At last I snatched them back and cried,
> "How can you be so slow?"

"My child," He said, "What could I do?
You never did let go."
(Written by Lauretta P. Burns.)

In life, so often we don't let go. I know I hate to delegate a task for fear that it is not completed to my liking and within time. Instead life can be like a parcel if you live in the present. The here and now is full of surprises. When Cooper and Polly were little I helped in school as a relief dinner lady. So called friends, with closed minds asked, "Why are you doing that? You don't need the money." The little voice in my head replies, "Why shouldn't I? Why, not?" I don't understand the logic of this. If you have humility you can see the benefit of any task. It is all about having the right attitude and the approach you take. Where else could I skip and play hop scotch without getting arrested again?

The children and teaching staff knew me and trusted me so I ended up counting the dinner money when the school secretary landed herself a new job. It was whilst I was playing secretary that Polly was assessed. She is such a bright shiny star and I thought it odd that she didn't seem to be retaining her spellings and reading seemed to be a real chore. The specialist lady arrived and asked for me, the secretary, to arrange for her to see Polly Price. In my role as secretary, I obviously didn't say that I was Polly's Mum. It was so strange that I was there at that moment. I felt as if I was in the right place at the right time and that there was simply no better place for me to be. Instead of waiting for a letter to reveal the results of Polly's assessment, I knew straight way. I could put the whole situation into context instead of just sitting at home waiting and fretting.

The assessment revealed that Polly is dyslexic. At

the time I felt that the situation was too cruel. I wasn't allowed to look after Katie as God had other ideas. Why then was I being trusted to make sure Polly has the best chance and given every opportunity? Surely, I deserve an easy life. I need to turn the situation on its head and realise that God only gives an individual what they are capable of dealing with. I suppose we should thank God for the challenges we overcome. There is little point asking "Why? Why me? Why us?" Surely it is better to ask "Why not?" Seize every challenge and make the most of every opportunity. Every cloud has a silver lining and, at some point, the sun will come shining through. Polly is a practical person and is very creative. She adapts and finds her own way of doing things to solve the immediate problem. I certainly know why she is my daughter!

I am not exactly sure when I wanted a "real" job again. I suppose it is a bit like needing a hair- cut. One day your hair is fine and you can style it easily, and the next day it looks a mess and you can't seem to do a thing with it. When I lived in Cardiff I always looked at the job adverts and sometimes I would send my CV just to let them know I exist. I usually say that I am not looking for a full time job, but I have the skills to work a couple of hours a week. Often I have created an opportunity for myself that fits like a glove. I believe that if you want something bad enough and you want it for the right reasons then you will attract what you want to you.

I work with unemployed teenagers and encourage them to take part in the world of work. I aim to work in partnership with the students and treat them with more respect than some of them have ever been shown. I aim to make a difference but realise that I am not going to get through to all of them. If I connect and get a result for one or two of them I guess we are doing well. Like the man on the beach throwing the star fish, stranded on the beach, back into the sea. The man was asked why he would want to undertake such a demoralising task, with so many star fish dying. He replied "It made a difference to that one, so it's worth doing." I ask myself if I ever make a difference. Sometimes I do. I remember the day John's mum phoned to say that he was poorly so wouldn't make it to class. She asked "Are you the lady who helps our John with his reading?" Like Cooper, John is into fishing and I took one of Cooper's cast off magazines in for him. This was enough to whet his appetite to bait his hook and for one very pleased Mum to say "It is wonderful to see our John picking up the paper!" Yes! Yes! YES!

I am always drawn to help the most -needy. If I was to foster a child I would choose the ones facing the most difficult circumstances. It is not just that I like a challenge but I owe it to Katie to make a difference whenever and wherever. I sometimes feel like the little boy in one of the stories in a Chicken Soup book by Jack Canfield.

One puppy was lagging behind. Immediately the little boy singled out the lagging, limping puppy and said what's wrong with that little dog? The store owner explained that the veterinarian had examined the little puppy and found that it didn't have a hip socket. It would always limp. The little boy became excited. "That's the puppy I want to buy." The store owner said "I'll give him to you." The little boy got quite upset and said "I don't want you to give him to me. That little dog is worth every bit as much as all the other dogs and I'll pay the full price. In fact, I'll give you $2.37 now, and 50 cents a month until I have paid for him."

The store owner countered "You really don't want to buy this little dog. He is never going to be able to run, jump and play with you like the other puppies." To this the little boy reached down and pulled up his pant leg to reveal a badly twisted, crippled left leg supported by a big metal brace. He looked up at the store owner and softly replied, "Well I don't run so well myself, and the little puppy will have someone who understands."

Through the tears and the sadness Katie has made a difference to the way I view the world. The little boy in the story viewed the puppies in his own special way. His damaged leg did that for him. I wouldn't be surprised if he was teased in school. I guess he protected school mates who were picked on and I bet it was a privilege for him to look after his chosen puppy.

From the bouts of depression I have suffered, the miscarriage and losing Katie I believe I am starting to understand my mission in life. Your mission is the foundation for the rest of your life. Who you are and what you do starts to fulfil an even higher purpose and you make a difference in the world. I could hardly drag myself out of bed and, when I was suffering with depression, I must have been a burden to Ivor. First and foremost I am a Mother and any work I take on board has to fit around this role. My work must be meaningful and worth getting out of bed for. The money I earn is of secondary importance. Each act we make is a statement about the purpose of our life. The soul pulls us towards our meaningful life. Our heart shows us our true feelings; where we want to go and what we want to do. The creative mind focuses on the bigger picture, helping us to rise above our fears and limitations. I guess that is why I'm typing and sharing and laughing and crying at the same time.

At the lowest points in my life I felt I made no difference and the world made no difference to me. At these times, when I feel I am taking instead of giving I usually turn to the poem "Footprints" by Margaret

Fishback. At the lowest points in my life God has carried me. God orders our steps and our stops. Even when we feel that we are walking a difficult path we are not alone:

"One night I had a dream
I was walking along the beach with my Lord
Across the dark sky flashed scenes from my life.
For each scene I noticed two sets of footprints in the
sand.
One belonging to me and one to my Lord.
When the last scene of my life shot before me
I looked back at the footprints in the sand.
There was only one set of footprints
I realise that this was at the lowest
And saddest times of my life.
This always bothered me and I questioned the Lord
About the dilemma.
"Lord you told me that when I decided to follow you
You would walk and talk with me all the way
But I am aware that during the most
Troublesome times of my life there is only
One set of footprints.
I just don't understand why,
When I needed you most you leave me."
He whispered, "My precious child, I love you
And will never leave you, never ever
During the trials and testings.
When you saw only one set of footprints
It was then that I carried you."

In Katie's album I have a lock of hair, a set of handprints and footprints' God is carrying me as I look at her footprints. God has allowed me to laugh when I see Polly measuring her hands and feet against Katie's. "My, what big feet she had!" says Polly. The story of

97

Little Red Riding Hood comes to mind and I grin, smile and laugh out loud. Polly's feet are growing. She will soon need new riding boots. Polly's footprints in the sand will be washed away. I often wonder where those little feet will take her. One day, if we have the same size feet we will be able to share our fashion shoes. Life is like a circle of footprints. The path leads from the centre to the centre, or as the Indians say, "From here to here." I am here and Katie is there. One day, as I draw my last breath I will meet Katie at her place. I will travel from here to there and the sky will be the limit for our reunion party. In reality there will not be a reunion because Katie is always with me. She is never far from my thoughts and she is a household name.

I don't think it matters whether you believe in God or not. My "take" on the situation is that God sends people into your life to support you just at the right time. My family and friend carried me when I was down. I didn't feel that I had the means to live but, I had a reason to live for. Cooper and Polly add meaning for me. I know that I sometimes spoil them and I understand that this is a reflection of my past. I believe that I am privileged to take care of these two people and I want to give them every opportunity in life. This often doesn't involve spending money but giving our time. It involves listening, understanding, encouraging and supporting their endeavours. Even when they want to do something risky you have to let go and let them sink or swim. They have to learn from their mistakes. If, by doing this, I am spoiling them then, "I am guilty your Honour!"

The Hero

We were so materialistic before Katie. We changed and started wondering when you get to be a hero in your life. Is it the day you start your own business or win a special contract. Maybe it is at the award ceremony when you are handed your certificate. It could be the day you get your first Mercedes Benz. How about when the Mercedes Benz breaks down or you lose that hard earned contract. At these moments can you extend to yourself the same concept of heroism you saw in Superman? Even when he is losing we have faith that Superman will win. Faith is a wonderful thing.

Ivor always wanted a Mercedes Benz so for Father's Day Cooper, Polly and I gave him the Janis Joplin CD containing the track entitled "Oh Lord Wont You Buy Me a Mercedes Benz?" Visualisation is a powerful tool, seeing and hearing makes you believe. For some seeing is believing. For others believing is seeing. Belief in yourself and belief in your dreams is vital.

Surprise, surprise Ivor used to drive a Mercedes Benz. He swapped the "Merc" for a sailing cruiser called Alchemy. The name "Alchemy" means changing base metal into gold. He already had gold as he had Cooper, Polly and I. In my opinion, the "Merc", boats and material things are just not important. I can hear you thinking, "That's fine for you to say because you may have these things." Things external to you may be very nice but they are transient. What is new will become old and the insatiable appetite of your ego requires constant feeding. You soon buy new to replace the old but not necessarily worn out. You are always changing – either regressing or progressing so you need to have inner strength. If you have strength within external, material things will lose their hold over you. You have to understand that I am partial to buying the odd hand bag and that will never change. Katie changed me and my outlook but my love of handbags remains intact.

Meditation and yoga give me inner strength and peace within. Space to grieve in peace and to just be myself. You don't need a boat or a "Merc" to meditate. You can replace or even fix a chair when it is broken. We couldn't replace or repair Katie when she got tangled in the cord. Never forget that you are human and you have to surrender to the fact that you can't control the bad things that happen to you. With the passage of time I sometimes pinch myself to check that I am real. Also to check that Katie's birth and death are real. In the beginning I thought about Katie on the hour and throughout every waking hour every day. I am not sure how much I slept but I regularly woke up with a start, thinking about my stay on the maternity ward. Today, I realise that it is lunchtime and I haven't thought about Katie. The whole experience feels unreal and then something, out of the blue will trip me up and catch me off guard. Our experience was sad but it was not all bad. How could it be when it has changed family, friends and virtual strangers so much?

Katie has been my greatest teacher. She is our "Super baby", not allowed to grow into a super lady on this earth. The only person you can control is yourself. You can control how you react to any given situation. It is better to respond than react. I regularly react or over-react so I have much to learn and the lessons are tough.

When you surrender the illusion of your control over external reality you not only admit to your helplessness to prevent bad things happening but you must, in truth know that you can't prevent solutions coming either.

Ivor was Polly's "Super Dad." Polly was due to go a skiing trip with the school. At the eleventh hour we realised that Polly's passport was out of date. The Post Office had already shut for the day and the bus was due to leave the school and head for the airport that evening. We could have beat ourselves up for being so stupid but, instead, we ripped into action, organised the passport and Ivor flew with Polly to Canada. This involved a flight change at Dallas and a seven hour trip in a four wheel drive vehicle across a glacier. They saw a wolf and Super Dad got Polly safely to Jasper. She missed only one day of the skiing trip and classmates and teachers clapped when she arrived. Ivor didn't do all of this because "the lady loves Milk Tray." He did it because people are more important than things. Polly was top priority and Ivor didn't hesitate to solve the problem. Katie made us think this way. Some people may think that we were mad and this was a total waste of money. All I can say that you have to make up your own mind and then live with the consequences of your actions. I am sure we will always check that our passports are in-date in the future as it is important to learn from our mistakes. I truly wonder how many dads would have travelled to Canada and stayed just one night. I think this was a test that Ivor passed with flying colours. I am sure that he will face other tests in the future. Let's hope he continues to make the grade and retain his "Super Dad" status.

I think that Ivor, Cooper, Polly and I have all passed many tests along the way. Our days are different and our tests or challenges cannot be the same. Katie is our common denominator. We all refer to her by name and she is remembered. Shopping with Polly one day she chooses a pale blue quilt cover for her bed. I try to talk her out of wanting it and she says "... but, it's designed by Katie Price, we have to buy. Straight out of the packaging and onto the bed with no time to spare and all because it was a Katie Price design. I don't have her photograph standing all alone for visitors to see. Some may be embarrassed and I protect them. Through my writing I am sharing her with the world but I don't want her photograph on display. It seemed a shame to keep her buried in her photograph album. Instead I made a collage of family photographs and quotations and Katie Price has pride of place in the bottom right hand corner. I can smile as I clean and walk past and others are spared any embarrassment.

Welcome Home

Have you ever sat thinking of someone and the phone rings and there they are. Maybe you meet someone you haven't seen for many years. A letter arrives or you meet just the right person to help you move on in life. This isn't strange. This isn't a coincidence, it is just the old saying "when the student is ready, the teacher appears" in action.

I have experienced this in life so many times and so have you. At the time I worked with a group of ladies and life had been cruel to them. I wanted to wrap them in a blanket of tender loving care – "a T.L.C. Blankey." Looking at my language you wouldn't think that I taught Basic English would you? I only have a handful of students and I do whatever I can to make them feel special and to boost their self esteem in the process. I never have to think too long or hard and I always follow their lead.

It was Mother's Day and their babies were too young to make cards so we made cards in the lesson and wrote a special message inside, from their baby. I believe it is important to "think outside the box" so we threw in a handful of marbles and pebbles in each baby bath followed by bubbles and with feet soaking and cuddling their babies we shared what we had written. I had no baby in my arms and I had not written anything but I wondered and baby Katie wasn't far from my thoughts. Our feet had been massaged and we took turns reading a selection of poems in praise of mothers. We chilled and shared our innermost secrets. When the time felt right I told them about Katie. They seemed to really appreciate this sharing and we found that we had lots in common. Some of them had lost babies for various reasons and so another common bond was formed within the group. They saw another side to the tutor. They realized that I was human and that we had all faced similar challenges. I had survived and they would survive, thrive and learn from life's lessons. I felt at home with the group and could truly be myself.

You probably think that I am weird but on the way home in the car I got to thinking that what we had been doing reminded me of Jesus, washing the disciples' feet at the last supper. I am not comparing myself to Jesus. He didn't use marbles and foot scrub, but that's how special the session felt. The lesson plan certainly looked different. I enjoy my work so much that it doesn't feel like work. I guess what I have just written doesn't sound much like work. I only work term time, three days a week so Cooper and Polly are not affected in any shape or form. You may think I was lucky to be in this situation but, it wasn't luck. I went out there and found work that fits like a glove.

In the group we had talked about the power of self esteem and feeling good about you. As a tutor I couldn't take them out for the day without a huge risk assessment which would not have given the go ahead. As a friend, two car loads and three babies, including my mum to help with the babies set off for the morning. We visited a local make- up factory shop and bought toys for us to play with after a beautiful lunch together. As I sit looking at the group photograph, with my mum in the front row, I feel privileged to have met and spent time with such fantastic characters. I surely learned as much from them as they learned from me.

Take it on faith that you can use everything that life sends your way. That includes the things you want and the things you don't want. When you stop pushing, driving and striving for things to be different you may find that things change anyway. I guess I want to help others because I have been supported and helped myself. The old adage what goes around comes around and the law of Karma comes into play. Whatever we do, good or bad, will come back to us. The law of cause and effect continues throughout our lives. The stars are in the sky all the time. It's just that we can only see them at night when it is dark. When life is dark we need to find a star, hold on to it and wish upon it. I guess my children are my stars. They certainly are little stars and I wish the best for them. What I really want is for them to be HAPPY with whatever life throws at them.

I arrive home from work and I can't get the nursery rhyme "Twinkle, Twinkle Little Star" out of my mind. I guess it's understandable after a day working with my Mothers and their precious babies. As usual my thoughts turn to Katie.

Twinkle, twinkle little star
Welcome home from afar.
Your face lights up our lives.
Your face lights up our living room.
Never stop twinkling, our little star.

I walk into the living room and find Polly flat out on the settee. Her friend is asleep on the other settee. They are covered with pretty, fluffy blankets and they look so peaceful in the dim light of the room. The blinds are open and the stars shine brightly in the clear night sky. In my mind's eye I see a bowling alley. God is ready to bowl and only one pin falls. The pin is my first son, baby Tom. You think God would let someone else have a turn but She or He bowls again. This pin is baby Katie. She was stillborn and the pin fell quietly. The next pin is my dad. He falls to the ground after a long illness and a heroic fight. God has gathered in all three of my precious pins. Please don't take any more, at least not just yet.

I realize why the image of the bowling alley is so vivid. I knew life with my dad for many years but I never knew life with Katie. She would be exactly a year older than Polly. Polly never knew Katie but at sixteen years of age, on holiday in Turkey she had a tiny tattoo of Katie's name on her wrist. Polly rides race horses and the tattoo is a constant reminder of her older sister. Polly says that when a horse is strong, Katie gives her the strength to deal with the horse. I have heard Polly tell people that she owes her life to Katie. If Katie had survived I would not have been pregnant just a month later. Katie lost her life and literally breathed life into her sister. Of their own accord my eyes begin to leak as the significance of this hits home.

The Christmas tree stands in the bay window. The lights are all white and they sparkle like tiny stars. I think back to the first Christmas after losing Katie. I didn't want to put up the decorations and trim the tree but I did for Cooper. Thank God for Cooper and his antics. The tree was up and back down again just as quickly as possible. Everything squashed back into the attic hoping for a better Christmas next year. Ivor and I went to the Christmas meal with the people I worked with. They were all so kind but I found it so painful listening to the Carols being sung. We left early and in the car I remember complaining to Ivor that listening to all the carols about babies was not a good experience. He looked at me and said "they are singing about baby Jesus, you know the words are going to hurt." It would have been easier if Christmas had been cancelled.

As I look at the two girls stretched out like elegant cats. I realize that this could have been Katie and Polly. Sharing a meal, sharing a living room, sharing clothes and lots of space. Home would have been busier but would life have been fuller? Would Polly and I be as close as we are today? We will never know but, there is little point regretting what we have never had and what was outside our control. We cannot control the life-changing events we have to face. As Mother Teresa says we are just like a little pencil.

"I'm a little pencil in the hands of God
Who is scripting his love letter to the world."
(Mother Teresa)

Sometimes I felt more like a puppet than a pencil. I certainly feel as if someone is pulling my strings and making me jump and dance. Sometimes I jump for joy bout other times I am prodded into action. If we are all pencils, what we write doesn't always feel like a love letter. Sometime I would like to be allowed to sleep peacefully in my pencil case.

Tom changed me.
Katie changed us all.
Katie changed us forever.
We are forever changed but the stars continue to twinkle.
Twinkle, twinkle little star
Welcome home from afar.
Your face lights up our lives.
Your face lights up our living room.
Never stop twinkling, our little star.
Katie, you don't have to be physically with us.
You operate from afar.

Tom, Katie and "Bamp" are on high.
Like three wise judges they sit and their light shines.
They light up our lives and they light the way.
God Bless all three twinkling, shiny pins.
It's a pity God has to bowl.
I would rather be a batsman than a bowler.
Just as well we don't get to choose the roles we play.

Rules to Live By

Katie opened my eyes and showed me the rules that are important to live a quality life. I fall way short of perfect but these are the values I try to live with, at least some of the time. Add your own or write your own that fit you perfectly.

1. Think before you speak. Ask yourself- is it true is it kind and is it necessary? Sometimes it is better to say nothing at all as actions speak louder than words.

2. Learn to listen more and talk less. This is why we have two ears and one mouth.

> "Learn to listen like a teddy bear
> With ears open and mouth closed tight.
> Learn to forgive like a teddy bear
> With arms open not caring who is right."
> (Unknown)

3. Forgive, don't bear grudges. Carrying past hurts weigh you down. Empty your rucksack and travel light. We all have baggage – is yours too heavy?

4. Please and thank- you cost nothing, so use them

and show respect to people.

5.   Share and show people you care. Smiles are free so give them away. You have to give before you get in life so be a giver and you will reap what you sow

6.   Before you can love others you have to learn to love yourself. If you don't even like yourself, how can you expect others to like you?

7.   What do you say when you talk to yourself? Do you shout at yourself and beat yourself up? When you talk to yourself do you imagine that you are talking to an old friend? If you do, you will be honest but still kind.

8.   Live for today. Yesterday is a spent cheque, tomorrow is a promissory note. The only cash you have is today.

9.   Live each day as if it is your last. If you knew today was your last day on earth, how would you spend it?

10.   Go with the flow. Life is like a river and you can't step in the same rive twice. It is essential that you are spontaneous and go with the flow

11.   There is no point worrying about anything outside your control. If you can change things then change them. If you can't make any changes then move on and there is no point worrying.

12.   Every word and deed of a parent is a fibre

woven into the character of a child which determines how that child fits into the fabric of society. It is your responsibility to watch your thoughts, words and actions.

13. The best thing you can do is to give your children roots to grow and wings to fly. Whatever you write on the heart of a child no water can wash it away.

14. Where you are in life is a result of your experience and what you've done up to now. Experience is the hardest kind of teacher – it gives you the test first and the lesson after.

15. Call people by name, not names. A microbe is a microscopic organism carrying a disease. Gossip is the most deadly microbe of all. It has neither wings nor legs, it is composed entirely of tales and most of them have stings!

16. Be interested in others. You can like almost anybody if you look for the good in them.

17. Be generous with praise and cautious with criticism. Make a sandwich of your criticism and make sure you butter it up.

18. What counts most in your life is what you do for others. Be alert to opportunities to help others. At the end of the day look back at what you've done during the day – especially the things that may have made a positive difference to someone else.

19. Everything is possible. Picture what you want

happening as if you are watching a film un-
fold. You are here for a reason. What are you
destined to do?

20. There are no rehearsals in life – enjoy the
journey.

21. Make changes from within. Make a difference
from within.

22. When you make a choice you change the
future. Make right choices for you.

23. When life throws you a lemon make lemonade.

24. Learn and grow from your mistakes.

"There is no oil without squeezing the olive
No wine without pressing the grapes
No fragrance without crushing the flowers
And no joy without sorrow."

(Unknown)

25. When you get to the end of your tether and you
just cannot cope any more, tie a knot in your
rope and hang on. The knot is called HOPE.
Never give up and always have hope in your
heart.

26. Do things right and do the right things.

27. Remember, it is nice to be important but, it is
more important to be nice.

28. It's as easy as A, B, C... There are 26 letters in

the alphabet. Katie didn't stay around to attend school and learn her alphabet. She has done much more. Through her brief appearance in my life she taught me her alphabet in her very own special way.

A - Avoid negative people, things and habits.
B - Believe in yourself!
C – Change your mind – it is ok to do so.
D – Don't give up and don't give in.
E – Enjoy today as it's all you have. Yesterday is gone and tomorrow isn't here yet!
F – Family and friends are treasures.
G – Give more than you planned to give.
H – Hang on to your dreams.
I – Ignore those who try to discourage you.
J – Just do it!
K – Keep on trying no matter how hard it seems.
L – Love yourself first and foremost.
M – Make it happen!
N – Nurture your spirit.
O – Open your eyes and see things as they really are.
P – Play more.
Q – Quitters never win and winners never quit!
R – Reach for the stars.
S – Speak your truth.
T – Trust in yourself and let your intuition guide you.
U – Understand yourself and your needs.
V – Visualise your dreams.
W – Wish upon a star.
X – Experience the moment.
Y – You are unique and nobody else on the planet is exactly like you.
Z – Zero in on your target and go for it!

The Epilogue

At The Seaside

"When I was down beside the sea,
A wooden spade they gave to me,
To dig the sandy shore,
My holes were empty like a cup.
In every hole the sea came up,
Till it could come no more."

(By Robert Louis Stevenson)

Saundershoe beach is deserted. All that remains after a day of play are a few sand castles, tiny footprints and the holes are filling. Soon the footprints will be lost forever.

Out to sea a surfer is trying to regain his balance. He looks behind and sees the next wave coming. You can't stop the waves so you have the option of watching from the beach or surfing. To ride the wave you have to be adaptable and go with the flow. It means waiting until the next wave comes along and then taking a chance. Set your goals in concrete and your plans in sand. Make the beach your goal. Be prepared to wipe out one set of footprints and replace it with another. Remember that "the journey of a thousand miles begins with a single step."(Lao Tzu – Chinese Philosopher). Take one more step. Check that it is in the right direction and write the next chapter in your book of life. If you can't see the next chapter, then at least turn over the page.

When we moved to Saundershoe my parents bought a house warming gift for us. It was a water sculpture of two people holding a ball. For me, the ball represents the world. Like Sleeping Beauty, Katie awoke me from a deep sleep. Losing Katie was a nightmare but, she opened my eyes to a world of new possibilities. The ball pivots on the water. The ball moves and life moves on. Life will never be the same again. The pebbles at the base of the sculpture are from Saundershoe beach. In between the pebbles there are glass butterflies and tiny stars. Don't be surprised that if I see them, I'll buy little glass roses to complete the dish. If you drop a ball it bounces. In life you have to learn to bounce. When things go wrong, as they do, you have to be resilient. There is no doubt that you must bounce back.

Your life is a journey. It has an outer purpose and an inner purpose. The outer purpose is to arrive at your goal or destination. It is so accomplish what you set out to do; to make a difference to people, to run a race, to travel the world, paint a picture or even write a poem or a book. Your outer journey or mission may contain a million steps. Your inner journey has only one step. That is the step that you are taking right now. As you become more deeply aware of this one step, you realise that it already contains in it all the other steps as well as the destination. This one step becomes an act of great beauty. Enjoy the moment and drink in the detail. Your light will shine as you fulfil your inner journey. As you journey within you will get to know your true self. As Lao-tse says "we must be childlike and live life in the moment, with our eyes wide open in wonder."

The song of the birds and the new green leaf greet you to their world. The morning tide comes in and the footprints disappear. The last slice of the moon calls goodbye and the sun climbs higher in the sky. Soon you'll see your shadow. The sound of the sea is the song in the background. Everywhere all the creatures are singing. All this is inside your heart as you take one more breath and face a brand new day.

Little baby Katie
Eyes of blue and lips of red.
6lb 2oz
Such a sweet, little thing.
Born and died on 13th September 1993.
It is so true
That all good things
Come in little packages.
My special delivery that September morn
Has changed me forever.
Katie was born.
Katie died.
KATIE MADE A DIFFERENCE.

"Good Night, God Bless, Katie."

Acknowledgements

Thank you to my family and friends
For their continuous support over the years and across the miles.

Thank you for all the medical staff who touched my life.

Thank you to FSID for making a difference at the lowest point in my life.

Thank you to Steve for his never- ending patience illustrating the book.

Thank you to the publishing company for their guidance and support.

Lightning Source UK Ltd.
Milton Keynes UK
UKOW05f1159181113

221304UK00001B/11/P